Strictly Business Body Language

Using Nonverbal Communication for Power and Success

Jan Latiolais-Hargrave

KENDALL/HUNT PUBLISHING COMPANY
4050 Westmark Drive   Dubuque, Iowa 52002

Dedication

To the Sisters who nurtured and educated me at Maltrait Memorial Catholic School, to my teachers at Kaplan High School, to my professors at the University of Louisiana who awakened my mind to learning and the power of knowledge and to my Cajun ancestry. These ingredients, in my "gumbo" of flavors, mark the magic that has helped me to treat others with the respect and dignity that I believe our Creator intended.

"There is hope for your future, says the Lord,
and your children shall come back
to their own country." (Jer. 31:17, RSV)

Contents

Introduction

The more times that I am asked by leading newspapers, magazines or television shows to comment on a person's body language, the more committed I become in my belief of the endless amount of information that can be gathered from watching a person and reading his nonverbal communication.

The story that remains in my mind of the accuracy with which we can read the behavior of another person through his body language happened several years ago. The *New York Post* had been known to contact me from time to time for my opinion of people and their behavior at current events around the globe. During Bill Clinton's televised testimony, it wasn't unusual for them to contact me several times a week for my take on Mr. Clinton's body language. They asked questions such as, "Is he lying?" "Is he being truthful?" "What does his nonverbal communication reveal about his inner-most thoughts?" "What does it mean when he bites his lower lip?" "What about when he crooks his eyebrow?"

On one particular Friday afternoon, a reporter from the *New York Post* called and asked if I would take a look at three pictures and give comments on each. She was writing a story on body language and was inquiring specifically about the placement of people's fingers and hands while they are seated. Of course I agreed, and told the reporter to fax me the pictures immediately.

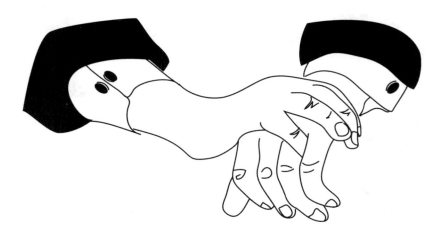

I informed her that my anology would be ready in fifteen minutes. She indicated to me that I would not be able to see the individual's faces or feet in the pictures, and also that she could not tell me if all three people were in the same room.

I imagined that these were people who had interviewed for jobs at the *New York Post* and figured that she wanted me to tell her which of the three was the most reliable, most honest and most suited for the job.

The first picture was that a man's hands. His hands were resting on his lap and were cupped together with his thumbs and little fingers twisted and intertwined. After studying the placement of his fingers, I carefully examined the photo for more information. I noticed that the man in the picture wore a suit and a shirt that required cufflinks. I made a note of the cufflinks because I thought they gave me insight into the individual's personality. A man who interviews for a job wearing a shirt that requires cufflinks gives off a different impression from a man who interviews for a job and wears a shirt that simply needs a button. This type of clue can reveal the level of position a person is applying for or it can give indications to the degree of vanity in the man himself.

The woman's hands in the second picture were comfortably placed on her lap. Her fingers were spread wide apart and her right hand was over her left hand. I noticed that she wore a pinkie ring

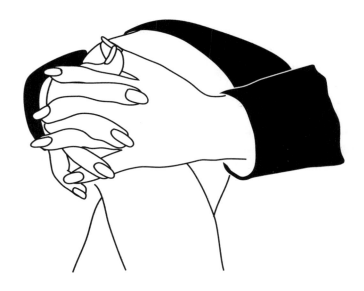

on her left little finger and was dressed in a suit. Her flat lap indicated to me that her legs were not crossed.

The third picture arrived quickly thereafter. It contained a woman's hands clasped together and held tightly in front of her, over her crossed knees. She was wearing a dark colored dress.

I made my notes then received the call from the Post reporter. She asked, "Do you have your analysis ready?" I said, "I certainly do!" She asked, "Well, what do you think about the guy?"

"Whoever this guy is, I wouldn't trust him as far as I could throw him." I replied. "I think that he has lied to you in the past and I feel that he will lie to you in the future." "In fact," I said, "I think that he's afraid of getting caught over something that he did." "He's nervous, uptight and holding back information." She said, "Wow, wait until I tell you who that is."

She then asked about the second person, the woman with her hands crossed on her lap. I told her, "She's the most honest of the three." "She's prim, proper, socially skilled and knows what she's talking about." "If I had to hire one of the three, you bet it would be this lady!" She said, "Wait until you find out who that is."

"What do you read from the third person's body language," she asked. "She's seated in a courtship gesture," I answered. "A lady tends to cross her legs toward a man who interests her and away from a man who does not." "She will then clasp her fingers together and hold on to her upper crossed leg, as she begins to feel more and more insecure." It is a gesture indicative of a lady desiring to hold on to the man she is with, but instead, clutches herself in an effort to look 'prim and proper.' I continued by saying, "She's very pensive and seems to be holding back information."

The reporter cut me off and excitedly said, "Stop, I must tell you who these people are." "You have hit the nail on the head." I said, "Who are these people?" She replied, "The first person is Marv Albert (the sports announcer), the first lady is Barbara Walters and the second female is currently dating Marv Albert."

In this book *you* will learn the language of the body and understand that every time you talk to someone your body supplements what you say with dozens of small gestures, eye movements, changes in posture and facial expression.

In the last twenty years, and increasingly in the last ten, a great deal of research has been carried out in nonverbal communication. In writing this book, I have summarized many of the studies by the leading behavioral scientists and have combined them with similar research done by people in other disciplines—sociology, linguistics, anthropology, education, psychiatry, family counseling, professional negotiating and selling. The book also includes many features developed from the countless reels of videotape and film that I have reviewed, plus some of my experiences and encounters with the thousands of people who I have interviewed, recruited, trained, managed and sold to over the past fifteen years.

To make it immediately useful as possible, I have extracted twenty-five basic rules for successful silent speech. These are explained in relevant chapters and also collected in the final chapter. If you are mainly interested in enhancing your silent speech sales skills as rapidly as possible, without concerning yourself on *how* and *why* each rule was formulated, then I suggest you turn directly to chapter eleven.

Silent speech is important to you. It significantly affects your chances of succeeding or failing in any encounter, whether personal or professional. Research suggests that only some 7 percent of the meaning in any conversation is contained in the words spoken. The majority of information is communicated by means of a complicated mixture of appearance, posture, gesture, gaze and expression. This offers a potent instrument of persuasion to those able to use it effectively and is especially important in situations where you suspect attempts to conceal stress, disguise deceptions or hide hostility.

The Table of Contents describes for you the topics that you can expect to encounter later in the book. Hopefully, this will help to convince you that it will be worth your while to persevere with your reading of the book and perhaps to participate in some of the practical exercises and experiments that are suggested in each chapter. My main wish, though, is that by the time you reach the end of the book, you will have a clearer idea of what is meant by the term 'body language,' what kinds of behavior it includes and also, from their omission, what kinds of behavior it is not meant to include.

The entire book considers the role of body language in personal development, with discussion to its role in the area of sales and interactive skills. It examines how effective use of body language can contribute to personal growth and better performance during sales negotiations. In addition, the role of body language in the development of synergic relations is explored, together with its role in establishing rapport, empathy and a sense of togetherness.

This book was originally intended as a working manual for salespeople, sales managers and executives, but any person, regardless of his vocation or position, can use it to obtain a better understanding of life's most complex event—a face-to-face encounter with another person.

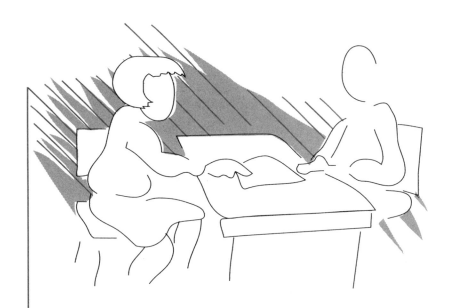

Mastering the Nonverbal Art of Selling: A Framework for Understanding

During the average 30-minute sales call, buyer and seller exchange approximately 800 different nonverbal messages, yet most salespeople focus only on the verbal part of the sale. Some listen to the tone of the voice—how the words are said, and some take literally each spoken word. Salespeople who pay attention to body language focus almost exclusively on facial expressions. Obviously, these are all necessary areas of interest. Words, the way they are spoken, and the speaker's face all give the seller information about how the sales call is doing. Voice and face, though, are only part of the picture. The body, the communication channel over which we have the least control, and understand the least, has the most impact.

Body Language Is Not New

Understanding the power of nonverbal communication will put you in excellent company. Man has used gestures since he appeared on earth. The Greeks were quite familiar with interpreting a man's character by watching how he carried himself and expressed his ideas with his body.

As far as the technical study of nonverbal communication goes, perhaps the most influential pre-twentieth-century work was that of Charles Darwin in 1872. His research spawned the modern studies of facial expressions and body language. Modern researchers around the globe have since validated Darwin's findings and observations. Dr. Albert Mehrabian, a noted researcher in the field of nonverbal communication, found that the total impact of a message is about 7 percent verbal (words only), 38 percent vocal (including tone of voice, inflection and other sounds) and a massive 55 percent through nonverbal expressions. Professor Ray Birdwhistell made some similar conclusions as to the amount of nonverbal communication that takes place among humans. He estimated that the average person actually speaks words for a total of ten or eleven minutes a day and that the standard sentence takes only about 2.5 seconds. Like Mehrabian, he found that the verbal component of a face-to-face conversation is less than 35 percent and that over 65 percent of communication is done nonverbally.

Researchers in the field of body language generally agree that the verbal channel is used primarily for conveying information, while the nonverbal channel is used for negotiating interpersonal attitudes, and in some cases is used as a substitute for verbal messages. Regardless of culture, words and movements occur together with such predictability, that Birdwhistell concluded that a well-trained person should be able to tell what movement a man is making by simply listening to his voice.

Charlie Chaplin and many other silent movie actors, pioneers of nonverbal communication skills, used this means to entertain and amuse many of us on the screen. Each actor was classified as good or bad as to the extent to which he could use gestures and other body signals to connect effectively.

Julius Fast published a summary of all nonverbal communication research done by behavioral scientists in a book in 1970. It was at that time that the public first became interested and aware of the existence and importance of body language.

Understanding nonverbal communication is not only necessary for individual success, it is also a vital part of a successful sales process. Since making selling easier and more rewarding is the goal for business, recently the sales industry has also decided on the value of understanding nonverbal communication selling power for increasing sales results, overcoming buyer resistance and boosting overall sales profits. History provides a dramatic example of how self-enhancing gestures and postures can lead to victory:

> After the legendary televised debate between the presidential candidates Richard Nixon and John F. Kennedy, the majority of the TV audience, based on positive body language, found Kennedy far superior to Nixon. The majority of the radio audience, however, judged Richard Nixon the winner of the debate.

In selling, some salespeople are still at the level of the candidate who had to learn about nonverbal communication through the school of hard knocks. Although most sales people know how to say the right things, they often lose the sale because of self-defeating nonverbal expressions.

Let that no longer be. Details to learning how to read another person's nonverbal gestures, from head to toe, are contained herein.

THREE STAGES TO INCREASED NONVERBAL SELLING POWER

Reading a prospect's body language is not the only goal in mastering nonverbal communication. Expertise in this area is usually gained, in phases, with time and practice. Three stages of awareness and skill are necessary before one becomes an expert in nonverbal selling power.

AWARENESS of THE BUYER: This stage involves learning the five major nonverbal communication channels and interpreting the buyer's nonverbal signals. It is a shorthand system of scanning the buyer for clusters of gestures. Instead of looking for specific movements or postures that 'mean' the client is bored, defensive or angry, a group of gestures from the five channels needs to be analyzed. These groups of gestures can indicate whether your buyer is open and receptive to your presentation, whether there are obstacles to your strategy that warn you to exercise caution, or they can alert you to stop and redirect your sales approach entirely.

AWARENESS of SELF: Your own nonverbal expressions can make or break a sale. Ask yourself: "How can I communicate in order to enhance the impact of my verbal selling skills?" "How am I perceived by the buyer?" "How can I avoid communicating self-defeating nonverbal signals during the call?" This stage requires roll playing and practice. Constructive criticism from peers and videotaping yourself in mock sales situations will show you how you look and act when your mind is concentrating on what you are saying. Once you understand your own nonverbal behavior, and how you use it to interact with clients, you are more aware of your impact on others.

MANAGEMENT of SELF AND BUYER: To reach this stage, you need to develop the ability to consistently apply your new nonverbal communication techniques together with your existing professional selling skills. Awareness and observation of the buyer and yourself will give you the ability to:

- spot negative nonverbal signals early in the sale;
- respond faster and more accurately to the buyer's nonverbal signals;
- increase your 'fluency' in managing your own nonverbal expressions;
- intensify your ability to combine verbal and nonverbal skills.

Body language reflects people's true feelings when they are unaware of their gestures. Your clients are visually telling you when they are uncertain, need more information, want a chance to ask questions or have strong objections—it's all in plain sight. And, so are your responses. You may mirror their emotions by making similar gestures, or take on a defensive posture in response to an objection. If they ask a question and you feel uncertain about how to answer, your body will be the messenger of your uncertainty.

Once you are totally aware of the buyer's movements and your gestures, you can put nonverbal selling power to work for you by managing your own and your client's body language.

How can you do this? By responding, instead of reacting, to your client's messages. It entails being friendly and positive, reassuring and understanding, both verbally and nonverbally. Exercise all 100 percent of your communications impact by using 55 percent of the message you send without opening your mouth.

Inborn, Genetic, Learned

Much research and debate has been done to discover whether nonverbal signals are inborn, learned, genetically transferred or acquired in some other way. Evidence collected from observation of blind and/or deaf people who could not have learned nonverbal signals through the auditory or visual channels and from observing the gestures and behavior of many different cultures around the world has aided in the findings.

The conclusions of this research indicate that some gestures fall into each category. For example, most children are born with the immediate ability to suck, indicating that this is either inborn or genetic. The smiling gestures of children born deaf and blind occur independently of learning or copying, which means that these must also be inborn gestures. When facial expressions of people from five widely different cultures were studied, it was found that each culture used the same basic facial gestures to show emotion. This led researchers to conclude that these gestures also must be inborn.

Speaking of inborn gestures, when you cross your arms on your chest, do you cross left over right or right over left? Most people cannot confidently describe which way they do this until they try it. Where one way feels comfortable, the other feels completely wrong. Evidence suggests that this may be a genetic gesture that cannot be changed.

It can be concluded that much of our basic nonverbal behavior is learned and the meaning of many movements and gestures is culturally determined. Most basic communication gestures are the same all over the world. When people are happy they smile; when they are sad or angry, they frown or grimace. Nodding the head is almost universally used to indicate 'yes' or affirmation. It appears to be a form of head lowering and is probably an inborn gesture, as deaf and blind people also use it. Shaking the head from side to side to indicate 'no' is also universal and may well be a gesture that is learned in infancy. When a baby has had enough milk, he turns his head from side to side to reject his mother's breast. The young child who has had enough to eat, shakes his head from side to side to stop his parent's attempt to spoon feed him and in this way, quickly learns to use the side-to-side head shaking gesture to show disagreement or a negative attitude.

GESTURE CLUSTERS AND CONGRUENCE

One of the most serious mistakes a novice in body language can make is to interpret a solitary gesture in isolation from other gestures or other circumstances. Similar to any other language, body language consists of words, sentences and punctuation. Each gesture is like a single word and a word may have several different meanings. It is only when you put the word into a sentence with other words that you can fully understand its significance. Gestures come in sentences and invariably tell the truth about a person's feelings or attitudes. The 'perceptive' person is one who can read the nonverbal sentences and accurately match them against the person's verbal sentences.

Incongruence of gestures occurs as we observe a speaker standing behind a lectern with his arms tightly folded across his chest (defensive) and chin down (critical and hostile), while telling his audience how receptive and open he is to their ideas. Or, he may attempt to convince the audience of his warm, humane approach all the while giving short, sharp karate chops to the lectern. Sigmund Freud once noted that while a patient was verbally expressing happiness with her marriage, she was unconsciously slipping her wedding ring on and off her finger. Freud was aware of the significance of this subconscious gesture and was not surprised when marriage problems began to surface.

Observations of gesture clusters and congruence of the verbal and nonverbal channels are the keys to accurate interpretation of body language. In addition to looking for gesture clusters and congruence of speech and body movements, all gestures should be considered in the context in which they occur. If, for example, someone is sitting at a bus terminal with his arms and his legs tightly crossed with his chin down and it is a chilly winter's day, it would most likely mean that he is cold, not defensive. If, however, a person used these same gestures while you were sitting across a negotiation table from him trying to sell him an idea, product or service, the gestures could be correctly interpreted as meaning that the person is negative or defensive about the situation.

Faking Body Language

A commonly asked question is, "Is it possible to fake your own body language?" The general answer to this question is "no" because of the lack of congruence that is likely to occur in the use of the main gestures, the body's micro signals and the spoken words. For example, open palms are associated with honesty, but when the faker holds his palms out and smiles at you as he tells a lie, his micro gestures give him away. His pupils may contract, one eyebrow may lift or the corner of his mouth may twitch. These micro signals contradict the open palm gesture and the sincere smile resulting in the receiver tending not to believe what he is hearing. Thankfully, the human mind seems to possess a fail-safe mechanism that registers *tilt* when it receives a series of incongruent nonverbal messages.

The face is used more often than any other part of the body to cover up lies. We use smiles, nods and winks in an attempt to cover up, but unfortunately for us, the body signals tell the truth. It is difficult to fake body language for a long period of time. The complexity with lying is that our subconscious mind acts automatically and independently of our verbal lie, so our body language gives us away. This is why people who rarely tell lies are easily caught, regardless of how convincing they may sound. The moment he begins to lie, his body sends out contradictory signals. It is these signals that give us our feeling that the person is not telling the truth. During the lie, the subconscious mind sends out nervous energy that appears as a gesture that can contradict what the person has just said. People whose jobs involve lying, such as actors and television announcers, have refined their body gestures to the point where it is difficult to see the lie, and onlookers fall for their stories, hook, line and sinker.

To deter us from spotting their lies, actors refine their gestures in one of two ways. First, they practice what 'feels' like the right gestures when they tell the lie. This is only successful when they have practiced telling numerous lies over long periods of time. Second, as difficult as it is to do, they eliminate most gestures while they are relaying the lie.

Try this simple test when an occasion presents itself. Tell a deliberate lie to an acquaintance and make a conscious effort to suppress all nonverbal gestures while your body is in full view of the other person. Even when your major body gestures are consciously suppressed, numerous micro gestures will still be transmitted. These micro gestures include facial muscular twitching, expansion and contraction of pupils, sweating at the brow, flushing of the cheeks, increased rate of eye blinking and numerous other microscopic gestures that signal deceit. Research using slow motion cameras shows that these micro gestures can occur within a split second. Usually only trained professional interviewers, salespeople and those whom we call highly perceptive are those who can consciously detect micro expressions during a conversation or negotiation. Results show that the most successful interviewers and salespeople are those who have developed the automatic ability to read the micro gestures during their face-to-face encounters with other people.

It is obvious, then, that to be able to lie successfully, you must have your body hidden or out of sight. Police interrogation involves placing the suspect on a chair in the open or placing him under lights with his body in full view of the interrogators; his lies are much easier to see under those circumstances. Naturally, telling lies is easier if you are sitting behind a desk where your body is partially hidden, or while peering around a closed door. The best way to lie is over the telephone!

How to Learn Body Language

Set aside at least fifteen minutes a day to study and read the gestures of other people, as well as acquire a conscious awareness of your own gestures. A good reading ground is anywhere that people meet and interact. An airport is a particularly good place for observing the entire spectrum of human gestures, as people openly express eagerness, anger, sorrow, happiness, impatience and many other emotions. Television also offers an excellent way of learning nonverbal communication. Turn down the sound and try to understand what is happening by first watching the picture. By turning the sound up every five minutes, you will be able to check how accurate your nonverbal readings are and before long it will be possible to watch an entire program without any sound and understand what is happening.

During the first few days of your awareness program in nonverbal communication, you may feel self-conscious and uncomfortable. You will be surprised to notice how many gestures you make, the way you sit, and how often you fiddle with objects or mask your facial expressions in response to a variety of situations. Relax. Enjoy your new knowledge and appreciate the competitive edge you will have once you move on to the management of these signals.

You may be asking yourself, "How will I ever be able to concentrate on what I'm saying and what my client is saying if I have to think about all of these other things?"

First, recognize that your subconscious mind is already an expert at body language. You are only training yourself to look for more nonverbal messages. Trust your intuition to make your impressions more accurate. A thorough understanding of body language allows you to be able to modify your own reactions and thus improve your sales calls.

Secondly, know that most people can hear at a rate of 400–500 words per minute, yet speak at a rate of 125–180 words per minute, about three times slower. Instead of becoming distracted during that extra listening time, use it constructively. Scan client signals; decide what messages they are sending out, and then plan your response.

Close Encounters: Territories, Zones and Awareness of the Five Major Channels of Communication

oving closer to a client so that you can scan him for nonverbal signals can be overdone. If you violate the buyer's 'intimate space,' usually a distance of up to 1¹/₂ feet, you are likely to get only negative readings.

Close Encounters

The amount of space a client needs to feel comfortable varies according to an assortment of factors. Cultural differences, age, sex, personality and the type of relationship you have with him all come into play. Generally speaking, Eastern Europeans, the French and Arabs prefer a much closer distance than British people do. Peers will tolerate a closer range of contact than people with a wide gap in age. Conversations between females will occur at closer range than male-female talks, and male-to-male encounters show the most distance. People who are outgoing by nature will want to be in a closer, friendlier position than those who are shy or aloof. Once you have worked with a client over a number of years, your speaking distance will be less than it would be if you were calling on a client for the first or second time.

Because of these differences, estimates for the amount of space a person will need in a given situation vary.

Intimate Space: Up to 1¹/₂ feet. Back off. This is too close for business situations.

Personal Space: 1–2 feet. Use for longtime clients, and only if *they* are comfortable.

Social Space: 4–7 feet. This distance allows room for stretching and gesturing without invading your client's territory.

Public Space: 10 feet or more. This is a good distance for delivering a speech or making small presentations.

Every country is a territory staked out by clearly defined boundaries and sometimes protected by armed guards. Within each country are usually smaller territories in the form of states and counties. Within these are even smaller territories called cities, within which are suburbs, containing many streets that, in themselves, represent a closed territory to those who live there. The inhabitants of each territory share an intangible allegiance to it and have been known to turn to savagery and killing in order to protect it.

A territory is also an area or space that a person claims as his own, as if it were an extension of his body. A person's own personal territory includes the area that exists around his possessions, such as his home which may be bounded by fences, the inside of his motor vehicle, his own bedroom or even his personal chair.

Along with his personal territory, man has his own private portable 'air bubble' that he carries around with him and its size is dependent on the density of the population where he grew up. This personal zone distance, which is culturally determined, tells others whether the person is accustomed to crowding or likes 'wide open spaces' and prefers to keep his distance from others.

Practical Applications of Zone Distances

While we will tolerate strangers moving within our personal and social zones, the intrusion of a stranger into our intimate zone causes physiological changes to take place within our bodies. The heart pumps faster, adrenaline pours into the bloodstream, blood is pumped to the brain and the muscles begin preparation for a possible fight or flight situation.

In other words, putting your arm in a friendly way on or around someone you have just met may result in that person's feeling negative toward you, even though he may smile and appear to

enjoy it so as not to offend you. If you want people to feel comfortable in your company, the golden rule is 'keep your distance'.

Crowding at concerts, movies, in elevators, trains or busses results in unavoidable intrusion into other people's intimate zones. Reactions to this invasion of personal space are interesting to observe. In Western cultures, people follow a list of silly, unwritten rules when faced with a crowded situation such as a packed elevator or bus. The rules include:

1. You are not permitted to speak to anyone, including a person you know.
2. You must avoid eye contact with others at all times.
3. You are to maintain a 'poker face'—no emotion is permitted to be displayed.
4. If you have a book or newspaper, you must appear to be deeply engrossed in it.
5. The bigger the crowd, the less body movement you are permitted to make.
6. In elevators, you are compelled to watch the floor numbers above your head.

Words such as 'miserable', 'unhappy' and 'despondent' have been used to describe people who travel to work in rush hour on the bus. These labels result because of the blank, expressionless look on the faces of the travelers, but they are misjudgments on the part of the observer. What the observer sees, in fact, is a group of people adhering to the unwritten rules that apply to the unavoidable invasion of their intimate zones in a crowded public place.

An angry mob or group of protesters fighting for a mutual purpose does not react in the same way as people do when their territory is invaded; in fact, something quite different occurs. As the density of the crowd increases, each individual has less personal space and takes a hostile stance. The size of the mob grows, each person becomes angrier and uglier and fighting usually takes place. Police, who try to break up the crowd so that each person can regain his own personal space and become calmer, use this information.

Only in recent years have governments and town planners given any credence to the effect that high-density housing projects play in depriving individuals of their personal territory. The consequences of high-density living and overcrowding are never ending. Overactive adrenal glands, resulting from the stress caused by the deprivation of each individual's personal territory as the population increases causes negative effects to the body's defenses.

In view of this, it is easy to see why areas that have the highest density of human population also have the highest crime and violence rates.

Police interrogators, to break down the resistance of criminals being questioned, use territorial invasion techniques. They seat the criminal on an armless, fixed chair in an open area of the room and encroach into his intimate and close intimate zones when asking questions. It takes only a short while for this territorial harassment to break down the criminal's resistance.

Management people can use this same approach to extract information from subordinates who may be withholding details, but a salesperson would be foolish to use this type of approach when dealing with customers.

Cultural, Country and City Factors Affecting Zone Distances

Americans who meet and converse stand at an acceptable 2 to 4 feet from each other and remain standing in the same place while talking. A Japanese person feels comfortable conversing with another person in a smaller 10-inch intimate zone. When an American and a Japanese person begin a conversation, it is as though they are slowly moving around the room. The American begins to move backwards away from the Japanese person and the Japanese person gradually moves towards the American. In their attempt to adjust to a culturally comfortable distance from each other, they give the impression that both are dancing around the conference room with the Japanese person leading. It is therefore obvious why, when negotiating business, Asians and Americans look upon each other with some suspicion. Sometimes Americans refer to Asians as 'pushy' and 'familiar' and Asians refer to Americans as 'cold', 'stand-offish' and 'cool'. The lack of awareness of the distance variation of the intimate zones for different countries can easily lead to misconceptions and inaccurate assumptions about one culture by another.

As previously mentioned, the amount of personal space required by an individual is related to the population density of the area in which he was brought up. Those who are brought up in sparsely populated rural areas require more personal space than those raised in densely populated capital cities. Watching how far

a person extends his arm to shake hands can give a clue to whether he is from a major city or from a remote countryside. City dwellers have a primate 18-inch 'bubble', the measured distance between wrist and torso when they reach to shake hands. People brought up in a country town, where the population is far less dense, may have a territorial 'bubble' of up to 4 feet or more.

Country people have a tendency to stand with their feet firmly planted on the ground and to lean forward as far as they can to meet your handshake, whereas a city dweller will step forward to greet you. People raised in remote or sparsely populated areas usually have a large personal space requirement, which may be as wide as 30 feet. Often, these people prefer not to shake hands, but to stand at a distance and wave.

City salespeople find this sort of information particularly useful for calling on farmers in sparse rural areas to sell farming equipment. Considering that the farmer may have a 'bubble' of 3 to 6 feet or more, a handshake could be a territorial intrusion, causing the farmer to react negatively and be on the defensive. Successful countryside salespeople unanimously insist that the best negotiating conditions exist when they greet the rural dweller with an extended handshake.

Like personal air space, property owned by a person or a place regularly used by him constitutes his private territory and he will fight to protect it. Such things as a person's home, office and car represent a territory because each has clearly marked boundaries in the form of walls, gates, fences and doors.

If the head of the house asks a visiting salesperson to be seated and the salesperson quite innocently sits in 'his' chair, the prospective buyer can become inadvertently agitated about this invasion of his territory and thus be put on the defensive. A simple question by the salesperson such as, "Which chair is yours?" can avoid the negative results of making such a territorial error.

Concerning zone knowledge, it is important to remember that others will invite or reject you, depending on the respect that you have for their personal space. This is why some secretly dislike the happy-go-lucky person who slaps everyone he meets on the back or continually touches people during a conversation. As a number of factors can affect the spatial distance a person takes in relation to others, it is wise to consider every criterion before making a judgment about why a person is keeping a certain distance.

Exploring the Five Channels

Since you are now aware of the important part spatial distances and nonverbal communication plays in a sales situation, monitoring your client's body language may not be as complicated as it seems. There are only five major nonverbal communication channels: body angle, face, arms, hands and legs that need to be explored fully.

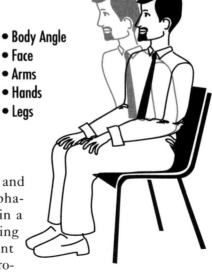

- Body Angle
- Face
- Arms
- Hands
- Legs

A quick scan of these five channels takes only seconds—quite a small amount of time to invest in improving your sales career.

Since a client's body language is most reliable when it changes from one gesture or stance to another, movement and intensity of these changes will be emphasized in detail and the role each plays in a sales situation. Eyes that stare, unblinking and undirected, say something different than eyes that move from you to your brochures during the business meeting. Legs that are crossed casually and remain still may not be a cause for concern until they are more tightly crossed, or a foot starts to swing, or the crossing is coupled with a shift in the client's body away from you. In any case, it is important to look for a cluster of gestures in any channel. A single gesture in one channel doesn't mean anything. That is why it is important to scan all five channels and use that information in a sales situation to increase your selling power. Although all five channels will be introduced here, they will be explained and examined in detail in the following chapters.

Channel One—Body Angle

An upright posture or a body movement directed toward you is an important clue signaling that the sale is headed in the right direction. Just as a client will sit closer to you if he feels comfortable and friendly, he will lean his body toward you if he is intent on listening to your presentation.

When a customer leans back or away from you, he is sending a negative message. By using the other channels you will be able to decide whether he is bored, angry, apprehensive or demonstrating superiority.

Show interest and a cooperative attitude toward your client by directing your body angle toward him. Back and forth motions indicate drive and a positive attitude. Avoid side-to-side movements because they suggest insecurity and doubt. Too much motion or complete stillness is likely to project nervousness or tension, so concentrate on using naturally flowing movements. And, if you get into a rhythm that matches your client's speech patterns, he will really feel that you are in step with what he is saying.

Channel Two—Face

There is more to a face than a smile. Although a client may hide his disinterest or disagreement behind a grin, his real feelings may be revealed in other ways.

Eye Contact—a customer will avoid eye contact if he is trying to cover up his true emotions, and gaze past you or around the room if he is bored. Increased eye contact signals honesty and interest.

Skin Color—a sudden flush or slowly deepening redness of your client's face sends out a vivid warning that something is wrong. Anger and embarrassment glow like a shiny red apple on some people.

Skin Tautness—tenseness and anger can be detected by looking for signs of tightness around the cheeks, jaw line and in the neck area. To understand this, try holding your breath and feel the increased stiffness in these areas on yourself. If you can consciously relax your facial and neck muscles when you begin to feel tense in a sales situation, you will feel more relaxed and make a better presentation.

Smiles—smiles that are genuine involve the whole face. If the rest of your client's body language tells you that he is open and interested, and that his smile is genuine, you can be sure that your presentation is hitting the mark.

Channel Three—Arms

Where your client puts his arms, how he moves them and the extent of his movements, will give you further information about his underlying attitude. In studying the arms channel, intensity is a key factor.

If the client has his upper arms and elbows as far back on his chair as they will go, and raises his hands into a 'stop' gesture, prepare for a defensive movement. The client who hangs one arm over the back of the chair will tend to also lean farther away from you, a negative reaction, or go to a hands-behind-the-head position of dominance. In either case, you do not have his full attention or acceptance. When the client has his arms well onto the desk as part of his overall body language—he is leaning forward and exhibiting interest in your proposal.

Arms are used to provide support for hand movements. Because of this connection, their position can give you advance warning of the hand signals that are likely to follow.

A client will use more arm movement when he is very involved in conveying an opinion. The broader and more vigorous the gestures, the more emphatic is the client's point. These can be positive, open gestures or angry threats.

Channel Four—Hands

There are thousands of hand gestures. How can you decide what your client's hands are revealing? By dividing these gestures into three main groups, you will get a general idea of whether the customer is reacting in a positive, cautious or negative way to your sales call.

1. Open and relaxed hands, especially when the palms are facing you, are a positive selling signal.
2. Self-touching gestures, such as hands on chin, ear, nose, arm or clothing, indicate tension. Probing for difficulties, or simply relaxing the pace of your presentation, may calm the client.
3. Hand gestures that contradict a facial expression indicate the client's true feelings. Watch for tightly clasped hands or fists.

It is very important for you to avoid self-touching and involuntary hand gestures during the sales call. No matter how calm or positive your words are, if the client senses tension or a negative reaction on your part, he will be on his guard and much less receptive to your presentation.

CHANNEL FIVE—LEGS

Most people believe that leg crossing is done for comfort. Did you ever stop to think about why people are comfortable in that position? Usually it's because their bodies are reflecting how they feel inside. A study of 2,000 people by Nierenberg and Calero in, *How to Read a Person Like a Book*, found that no sales were made while the participants had their legs crossed. Even if all other channels appear to be open and positive, the customer who keeps his legs crossed may have some minor reservations that will prevent you from completing the sale if these uncertainties are not uncovered and unanswered.

A client who keeps his feet on his desk, is displaying an attitude of ownership and dominance. It says, "Go ahead and try to sell me." Crossed legs or crossed ankles signal that there is something preventing a completely open mind. The client is probably feeling defensive or reserved and tends to be uncooperative. On the other hand, uncrossed legs send a message of cooperation, confidence and friendly interest in the other person.

When the client's legs are crossed away from you, his body is usually also shifted away from you and the sales call is not going well. Although it is best not to cross your legs at all, a leg crossed towards the client is acceptable in the early phase of a sale. If the client mirrors the legs crossed towards you position, he is feeling that the two of you are alike and tuned in to each other.

Clustering and Consistency

A single gesture is like a word standing alone. Without a sentence to give it a context, you can't be sure of its meaning. Clusters of gestures are the sentences and paragraphs of body language. A puzzled facial expression shows you only part of what your client is thinking. Does he need more information? Is there something you said that contradict something he's heard from another company? Paying attention to his other nonverbal communication channels will give you a clearer indication of his feelings. If he is puzzled and positive, you'll want to act one way. If he is puzzled and negative, your approach will go in another direction.

Increasing Your Nonverbal Selling Power

Your goal in increasing your nonverbal selling power lies in:

* Selecting the appropriate distance—allowing enough space for the buyer to feel comfortable.
* Scanning the buyer's five nonverbal communication channels—body angle, face, arms, hands, legs—so that you can easily decide on the most effective verbal and nonverbal response strategy.

The worst thing a seller can do is mimic a buyer's negative signals or react to the client with anything but positive, helpful nonverbal messages. Making the most of this new knowledge allows you to proceed with confidence from the opening of the sale to the successful close.

The body language of failure—no eye contact, fidgeting, nervousness, defensiveness, confrontation and poor posture—are interpreted as the nonverbal messages of fear, weakness or discontent.

The body language of success—good eye contact, a comfortable, erect body posture, and open gestures that move toward the buyer—are signals that give the impression of power, confidence and satisfaction.

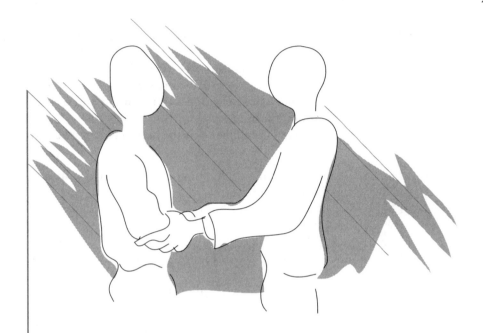

The Hidden Power of Your Handshake: Palm Gestures

Throughout history, the open palm has been associated with truth, honesty, allegiance and submission. Many oaths are taken with the palm of the hand over the heart. The palm is held in the air when someone is giving evidence in a court of law; the Bible is placed in the left hand and the right palm is proudly held up for the members of the court to view.

Palms touch together during handshakes. By using the handshake correctly during the first moment of physical contact with another person, you can, in less than five seconds, confirm an already favorable impression or do much to correct an initially unfavorable one. The handshake provides us with direct and immediate information about another person.

During the course of a handshake, information is conveyed in six ways:

1. The appearance of the hand: the length, shape and cleanliness of the palm, fingers and nails.
2. The texture of the grip: whether the hand is soft and delicate or hard and rough.
3. The degree of dryness or dampness.
4. The amount of pressure used: ranging from overly strong to insufficiently firm.
5. The time spent in contact with the other person: by increasing or decreasing the time spent shaking hands from the average five seconds, the meaning of the handshake is significantly changed.
6. The style of grip: the dominant style, the submissive style and the double-hand grip each convey a different message.

Openness and Honesty

In sales encounters, people use two basic palm positions. The first has the palm facing upwards. The second has the palm facing down as if it is restraining something. Upward-facing palms signify acceptance, while downward-facing palms signify control.

One of the most valuable ways of discovering whether a client is being open and honest or distrustful is to look for palm displays. For example, when someone wishes to be totally open or honest, he will hold one or both palms out to the other person and say something such as, "Let me be completely open with you." When someone begins to open up or is truthful, he will expose all or part of his palms to another person. Like most body language, this is a

completely subconscious gesture, one that gives you a feeling or hunch that the other person is telling the truth. When a child is lying or concealing an object, his palms are hidden behind his back. Similarly, a person who wants to conceal his whereabouts after a night out with friends will often hide his palms in his pockets or in an arm-fold position when he tries to explain where he was. Thus, the hidden palms give the impression that someone is holding back the truth.

During a sales negotiation, it is wise to look for the customer's open palms when he gives reason why he cannot buy the product, because only valid reasons are given with exposed palms.

It is possible to make yourself appear more credible by practicing open palm gestures when communicating with others; conversely, as the open palm gestures become habitual, the tendency to tell untruths lessens. Interestingly, most people find it difficult to lie with their palms exposed. The use of palm signals can, in fact, help to suppress some of the false information others may give and it also encourages them to be open with you. Briefly placing your right hand over your heart as you speak signals honesty.

Palm Power

The human hand gives one of the least noticed, but most powerful nonverbal signals. When used correctly, palm power invests its user with a degree of authority and the power of silent command over others. To understand handshake styles, let's first explore palm command gestures.

There are three main palm command gestures: the palm-up position, the palm-down position and the palm-closed-finger-pointed position. The differences of the three positions can perhaps be shown in this example: suppose that you ask someone to pick up a box and carry it to another location in the same room. Assume that you use the same tone of voice, the same words and facial expressions and change only the position of your palm as you request the box to be moved.

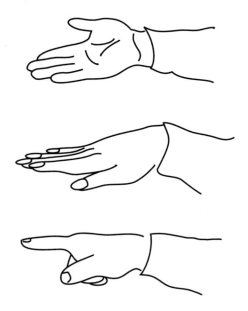

The palm facing up is used as a submissive, non-threatening gesture, reminiscent of the pleading hand of a street beggar. The person being asked to move the box will not feel that the request is given with pressure and, in a normal superior/subordinate situation, will not feel threatened by the command.

When the palm is turned to face downwards, you will have immediate authority. The person to whom you have directed the request feels that he has been given an order to remove the box and may feel antagonistic towards you, depending on your relationship with him. For example, if the person to whom you gave the request was a co-worker of equal status, he could reject your palm-down request and would be more likely to carry out your wish if you had used the palm-up position. If the person to whom you give the request is your subordinate, the palm-down gesture is acceptable, as you have the authority to use it.

Once the palm is closed into a fist with the pointer finger extended, the pointed finger becomes a symbolic club with which the speaker figuratively beats his listener into submission. The pointed finger is one of the most irritating gestures that a person can use while speaking, particularly when it beats time to the speaker's words. If you are a habitual finger-pointer, try practicing the simple palm-up or palm-down position and you will find that you create a more relaxed attitude and have a more positive effect on other people.

Dominant and Submissive Handshakes versus Vertical Handshakes

Shaking hands is a relic of the caveman era. Whenever cavemen met, they would hold their arms in the air with their palms exposed to show that no weapons were being held or concealed. This palms-in-air gesture became modified over the centuries and such gestures as the palm raised in the air, the palm over the heart and numerous other variations developed. The modern form of this ancient greeting ritual is the interlocking and shaking of the palms, which in most English-speaking countries, is performed both on initial greeting and on departure. The hands are normally pumped three to seven times during the hand-shaking ritual.

Assume that you have just met a client for the first time and you greet each other with a customary handshake. One of three basic attitudes is transmitted through the handshake. There is dominance: 'I can dominate this person. He will do as I wish', submission: 'This person is trying to dominate me. I'd better be cautious', and equality: 'I like this person. We will get along well together'.

These attitudes are transmitted subconsciously and, with practice and conscientious application, proper handshake techniques can have an immediate effect on the outcome of a sales encounter.

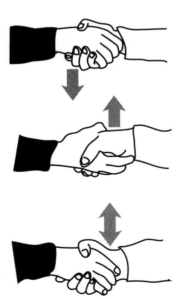

Turning your hand so that your palm faces down in the handshake transmits dominance. Your palm need not be facing the floor directly, but should be facing downwards in relation to the other person's palm. This tells him that you wish to take control in the encounter that follows. Studies of fifty-four successful senior management people have revealed that not only did forty-four initiate the handshake, but they also used dominant handshake control.

Just as the dog shows submission by rolling on its back and exposing its throat to the aggressor, so the human uses the palm-up gesture to show submission to others. The reverse of the dominant handshake is to offer you hand with your palm facing upwards. This is particularly effective when you want to give the client control or allow him to feel that he is in command of the sales meeting.

When two dominant people shake hands, a symbolic struggle takes place as each person tries to turn the other's palm into the submissive position. The result is a vice-like handshake with both palms remaining in the vertical position as each person transmits a feeling of respect and rapport to the other.

When you receive a dominant handshake from another person, it is not only difficult to force his palm back over into the submissive position, but it becomes very obvious when you do it. There is a simple technique for disarming the dominant handshake that, in addition to giving you back the control, can enable you to intimidate the other person by invading his personal space. To perfect this disarmament technique, you need to practice stepping forward with your left foot as you reach to shake hands. Next, bring your right leg forward, moving in front of the person and into his personal space in order to complete the maneuver, and then shake the person's hand. This tactic allows you to straighten the handshake position or to turn the other person's hand into the submissive position. It also allows you to take control by invading the other person's intimate zone.

Analyze your own approach to shaking hands to determine whether you step forward on your left or right foot when you extend your arm to shake hands. Most people are right footed and therefore, at a great disadvantage when they receive a dominant handshake, as they have little flexibility or room to move within the confines of the handshake and it allows the other person to take control. Practice stepping into a handshake with your left foot and you will find that it is quite simple to neutralize a dominant handshake and take control.

Another simple maneuver to counter the palm-down thrust is to grasp the person's hand on top and then shake it. With this approach, you become the dominant party, as you not only have control of the other person's hand, but your hand is in the superior position, on top of his with your palm facing down. As this can be embarrassing to the aggressor, it should be used with caution and discretion.

Hands placed and left in a vertical position during a handshake signal 'equal opportunity' negotiations for both parties involved.

HandshakE STylES

The glove handshake is sometimes called the politician's handshake. The initiator tries to give the receiver the impression that he is trustworthy and honest, but when this technique is used on a person he has just met, it has the reverse effect. The receiver feels suspicious and cautious about the initiator's intentions. The glove should only be used with people to whom the initiator is well known.

Few greeting gestures are as uninviting as the dead fish handshake, particularly when the hand is cold or clammy. The soft, placid feel of the dead fish makes it universally unpopular and most people relate it to weak character, mainly because of the ease with which the palm can be turned up. Surprisingly, many people who use the dead fish are unaware that they do so, therefore it is wise to ask your friends to comment on your own handshake delivery.

The knuckle grinder is the trademark of the aggressive 'tough guy' type. It is too abrasive to use during a sales call and unfortunately, there is no effective way to counter it, apart from a verbal comment about it.

Like the palm-down thrust, the stiff-arm thrust tends to be used by aggressive types. Its main purpose is to keep you at a distance and out of the initiator's intimate zone. People brought up in rural areas who have a larger intimate zone to protect their personal territory also use it. With rural dwellers, however, there is a tendency to lean forward or even balance on one foot when delivering the stiff-arm thrust.

The fingertip grab is like the stiff-arm thrust that has missed the mark; the user mistakenly grabs the other person's fingers. Even though the initiator may appear to have a keen and enthusiastic attitude toward the receiver, in fact he lacks confidence in himself. Like the stiff-arm thrust, the main aim of the fingertip grab is to keep the receiver at a comfortable spatial distance.

Pulling the receiver into the initiator's territory can mean one of two things; first, the initiator is an insecure type who feels safe only within his own personal space or second, the initiator is from a culture that has a small intimate zone and he is behaving normally.

The intention of the double-handed handshake is to show sincerity, trust or depth of feeling towards the receiver. Two significant elements should be noticed. First, the left hand is used to communicate the extra feeling that the initiator wishes to transmit and its extent is related to the distance that the initiator's left hand is moved up the receiver's right arm. The elbow grasp transmits more feeling than the wrist hold, and the shoulder hold transmits more sentiment than the upper-arm grip. Second, the initiator's left hand represents an invasion into the receiver's intimate and close intimate zones. In general, the wrist hold and the elbow grasp are acceptable only between close friends or relatives and in these cases; the initiator's left hand penetrates only the receiver's intimate zone. The shoulder hold and the upper-arm grip enter the receiver's close intimate zone and may involve actual body contact. They should be used only between people who experience a close emotional bond at the time of the handshake. Unless the extra feeling is mutual or the initiator has a good reason for using a double-handed handshake, the receiver will become suspicious and mistrust the initiator's intentions. It is quite common to see politicians greeting voters and salespeople meeting their new customers with

a double-handed handshake without re-
alizing that this can be social suicide,
putting the receiver off.

WHO REACHES FIRST?

Although it is a generally accepted cus-
tom to shake hands when meeting a person for the first time, there are some circumstances in which it may be unwise
for you to initiate the handshake. Considering that a handshake is a sign of
welcome, it is important to ask yourself
several questions before you initiate
one: "Am I welcome?" "Is this person
glad to meet me?" Sales trainees are cau-
tioned that, if they initiate the handshake with a buyer on whom they call
unannounced and uninvited, it can produce a negative result as the buyer may
not want to welcome them and is forced
to do something that he may not want to
do. It is important to note that people
with arthritis and those whose hands are
their profession may become defensive
if they are forced to shake hands. Under
these circumstances, someone in sales
would be wise to wait for the other person to initiate the handshake and, if not
forthcoming, to nod as a sign of greeting.

Use the following guidelines to
achieve a friendly handshake and access
to your client's attitudes and emotions
early in your opening.

1. Keep your hand in a vertical
   (straight up and down) position—
   palm down communicates a dominant attitude; palm up communicates a submissive demeanor.
2. Apply moderate pressure—overly forceful handshakes (bone-
   crushers) convey aggression and a lack of consideration; limp
   handshakes (dead fish) convey insecurity, or lack of interest.

3. Move your arm at a moderate pace—quick, jerky, overly enthusiastic hand pumping sends all but the most familiar clients into retreat; no movement at all shows a lack of energy and cooperativeness.
4. Pay attention to how your client returns your handshake—all of these interpretations apply to clients too!

YOUR PRICE IS TOO HIGH:
HAND AND ARM
GESTURES

What does *your* body communicate when your prospect says: "Your price is too high?" Think of your last sales call and try to remember specifics—your body angle, facial expressions, the position of your arms, hands and legs. Most salespeople show negative changes in their body posture when hearing objections.

When a client sees signals such as crossed arms and legs, head scratching, swaying from side to side, nose rubbing and fingers under the collar, your problems are intensified. The prospect may think: "Ah, now I've come to the weak spot!" Even though your verbal reply is flawless, your nonverbal expressions may communicate: "I'm uncomfortable about this," or "I don't know if I will be able to convince you about buying from me."

Salespeople who communicate negative nonverbal signals after hearing the prospect's objections fail to recognize that 99 percent of all customer objections are preceded by negative body language gestures. For these reasons, it can be easily understood why positive gestures on the part of the salesperson are absolutely necessary the moment he notices a customer's objections. It is far better to deal with problems early. As soon as the salesperson notices the first disapproving nonverbal signal, it should be managed and responded with open, concerned gestures in efforts to salvage the situation.

Rubbing the Palms Together

Rubbing the palms together is a way in which people nonverbally communicate positive expectation. The dice thrower rubs the dice between his palms as a sign that he expects to win, the master of ceremonies rubs his palms together and says to his audience, "We have long looked forward to hearing our next speaker," and the excited salesperson struts into the sales manager's office, rubs his palms together and says excitedly, "We've just received a huge order, boss!" However, the waiter who comes to your table at the end of the evening quickly rubbing his palms together and asking, "Anything else, sir?" is nonverbally telling you that he is expecting a tip.

The speed at which a person rubs his palms together signals what he's thinking and feeling. For example, you want to buy a home and you go to see a real estate agent. After describing the property you are seeking, the agent rubs his palms together quickly and says, "I've got just the right place for you!" The agent has signaled that he expects the results to be to *your* benefit. But how would you feel if he rubbed his palms together very slowly as he told you that he had the ideal property? He would then appear to be cunning or devious and would give you the feeling that the expected results would be to *his* advantage rather than yours. Salespeople are taught that if they use the palm-rub gesture when describing products or services to prospective buyers, they should be certain to use a fast hand action to avoid putting the buyer on the defensive. When the buyer rubs his palms together and says to the salesperson, "Let's see what you have to offer!" it is a signal that the buyer is expecting to be shown something good and is likely to make a purchase.

A word of warning: a person who is standing at a bus terminal in freezing winter conditions and who rubs his palms together briskly may not necessarily be doing this because he is expecting a bus. He does it because his hands are cold!

Thumb and Finger Rub

Rubbing the thumb against the fingertips or against the index finger is commonly used as a money expectancy gesture. Some salespeople use it while saying to their customers, "I can save you 40 percent." It is also customary to rub the index finger and thumb together and say to a friend, "Lend me ten dollars." It is not a suitable gesture during negotiations and is obviously a sign that should be avoided at all times by professional people when dealing with clients.

Hands Clenched Together

At first this seems to be a confidence gesture as people who use it are often smiling and sound happy. Research on the hands-clenched position concludes that it is a frustration gesture, signaling that the person doing it is holding back a negative attitude and is somewhat fright-

ened. The gesture has three main positions; hands clenched in front of the face, hands resting on a desk or on the lap when seated and thirdly, hands placed in front of the crotch when standing.

There also appears to be a correlation between the height at which the hands are held and the strength of the person's negative mood; that is, the higher the hands are held, the more difficult the person would be to handle. Like all negative gestures, some action needs to be taken to unlock the person's fingers to expose his palms and the front of his body, or the hostile attitude will remain. In these cases, it would be wise for the salesperson to hand something to the client; a book or a pamphlet, causing the client's clenched hands to drop as he picks up the object and thus becomes more open in his body language.

Hands Steepled Together

Fingertips that touch describe the steeple position, and it is one gesture that can be understood and interpreted in isolation from other gestures. People who are confident, superior types or who use minimal, restricted body gestures often use this signal, and, by doing so, they convey their self-assured attitude.

This fascinating gesture is frequently used in superior/subordinate interactions to indicate an assertive or 'know-it-all' attitude. Managers will use this position while giving instructions or advise to subordinates.

The gesture has two versions, the raised steeple, the position usually taken when the steepler is giving his opinions or ideas and is doing the talking. The lowered-steeple gesture is normally used when the steepler is listening rather than speaking. When the raised-steeple position is taken with the head tilted back, the person tends to assume an air of smugness or arrogance.

Although the steeple gesture is a positive signal, it can be used in either positive or negative circumstances and may be misunderstood. For example, a salesman presenting his product to a potential buyer may have observed several positive gestures (open palms, head up, body leaning forward) given by the buyer during the interview, then notice the steeple position. If the steeple follows a series of other positive gestures, appearing when the salesperson shows the buyer the solution to his problem, the salesman has been given a cue to close the sale and should ask for the order and expect to get it.

On the other hand, if the steeple gesture follows a series of negative gestures (arm folding, leg crossing, looking away and numerous hand-to-face gestures), and is done towards the close of the sales presentation, the buyer is signaling that he is confident he will not buy or that he can easily get rid of the salesman. In both these cases the steeple gesture means confidence, but one has positive results and the other negative consequences for the salesperson. The movements preceding the steeple gesture are the key to the outcome.

Gripping Hands, Arms and Wrists

Prominent male members of the British Royal Family are noted for their habit of walking with their heads up and chin out while gripping one palm with the other palm behind the back. This gesture is also used by the policeman patrolling his beat, the principal of the local school when he leisurely walks through the schoolyard, senior military personnel and others in positions of authority.

It is a superiority/confidence gesture position that allows the person doing it to express his vulnerable stomach, heart and throat regions to others in a subconscious act of fearlessness. It has been proven that if you take this position when you are nervous and in a high-stress situation, you can begin to feel relaxed, confident and even authoritative.

The palm-in-palm gesture should not be confused with the hand-gripping-wrist gesture which is a signal of frustration and an attempt at self-control. In this case, one hand tightly grips the other wrist or arm as if it is an attempt by one arm to prevent the other from striking out.

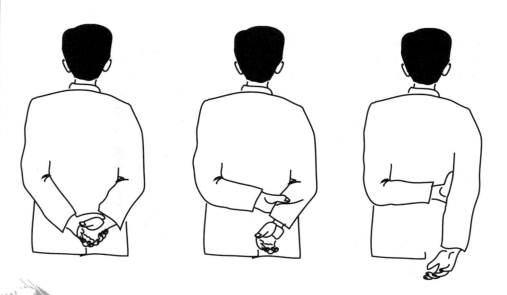

Interestingly, the further the hand is moved up the back, the angrier the person is becoming. It is this type of gesture that has given rise to the expression, "Get a good grip on yourself." Salespeople calling on a potential buyer who have been asked to wait in the buyer's reception area often use this gesture. It is a poor attempt by the salesman to disguise his nervousness and anger. If this self-control gesture is changed to the palm-in-palm position, a calming and confident feeling can result.

Thumb Displays

In palmistry, the thumbs denote strength of character and ego. The nonverbal use of thumbs agrees with this. Exposed thumbs grasping jacket lapels are used to express dominance, superiority or even aggression. Thumb displays are positive signals and are used in the typical pose of the 'cool' manager in the presence of his subordinates.

Hand Parade

There are thousands of hand gestures. How can you decide what your client's hands are revealing? Divide hand gestures into three main groups and you will get a general idea of whether the customer is reacting in a positive, cautious or negative way to your sales call.

1. Open and relaxed hands, especially when the palms are facing you, are a positive selling signal.
2. Self-touching gestures, such as hands on chin, ear, nose, arm or clothing, indicate tension. Probing for difficulties, or simply relaxing the pace of your presentation may calm the client.
3. Involuntary hand gestures, especially if they contradict a facial expression, indicate the client's true feelings. Watch for tightly clasped hands or fists.

Remember to avoid self-touching and involuntary hand gestures during your sales call. No matter how calm or positive your words are, if the client senses tension or a negative reaction, he will be on his guard and much less receptive to your presentation.

HEAR, SPEAK AND SEE NO EVIL: HAND-TO-FACE GESTURES

How can you tell when someone is lying? Recognition of the nonverbal deceit gestures can be the most important sales observation skills you can acquire. There are two methods of lying: to *conceal* and to *falsify*. In concealing, the liar withholds some information without actually saying anything untrue. In falsifying, an additional step is taken; not only does the liar withhold true information, but he also presents false information as if it were true.

When there is a choice about *how* to lie, liars usually prefer concealing to falsifying. There are many advantages. For one thing, concealing usually is easier than falsifying. Nothing has to be made up and there is no chance of getting caught without having the whole story worked out in advance.

Concealment lies are easier to cover afterward if discovered. The liar does not go as far out on a limb and has many available excuses—ignorance, the intent to reveal later, memory failure and so on. The person who says, "to the best of my recollection" provides an out if later faced with something he has concealed. If the truth later comes out, the liar can always claim not to have lied about it, that it was just a memory problem.

Deceit, Doubt, Lying

One of the most commonly used symbols to defy deceit is that of the three wise monkeys who hear, speak and see no evil. Their hand-to-face actions form the basis of the human deceit gestures. In other words, when we see, speak and hear untruths or deceit, we often attempt to cover our mouth, eyes or ears with our hands. Children use these obvious deceit gestures quite openly. If a young child tells a lie, he will often cover his mouth with his hands in an attempt to stop the deceitful words from coming out. If he does not wish to listen to a reprimanding parent, he simply covers his ears with his hands. When he sees something he doesn't wish to look at, he covers his eyes with his hands or arms. As we grow older, our hand-to-face gestures become more refined and less obvious but they still occur when we're covering up, witnessing doubt or exaggerating the truth.

Hand-to-face gestures should not be interpreted in isolation of other gestures. Someone using a hand-to-face gesture doesn't always guarantee that he is lying to you. It can, however, indicate that the person is uncomfortable about deceiving you or what he is saying and further observation of his other gesture clusters can confirm your suspicions.

In most instances, the hand-to-face gestures associated with deceit are done with the left hand. It is not to indicate that a left-handed individual would lie more than a right-handed person. Reasoning for this lies in the fact that the left hand is operated by the right, creative side of the brain and since a person's right brain activity is more so associated with ingenuity and imagination, words and thoughts stored there are easier to be brought out, or 'come to life,' when the speaker uses his left hand. It is further substantiated by the fact that throughout our lives we are taught to associate the left hand with bad or negative movements and connect the right hand with good or positive gestures. History has shown that in some countries, the left hand is so associated with negativity that it cannot be placed on the dining table; it is strictly used for wiping purposes.

THE MOUTH GUARD

The mouth guard is one of the few adult gestures that is as obvious as if a child were doing it. The hand covers the mouth and the thumb is pressed against the cheek as the brain subconsciously instructs it to try to suppress the deceitful words that are being said. Sometimes this gesture may only be several fingers over the mouth or even a closed fist over the mouth, but its meaning remains the same.

People try to disguise the mouth-guard gesture by giving a fake cough. When playing the role of criminal, Humphrey Bogart often used this gesture when discussing criminal activities with other gangsters or when being interrogated by the police to show nonverbally that he was being dishonest.

If the person speaking repeatedly uses this gesture, it indicates that he is uncomfortable about the information coming from his mouth and is usually telling a lie. If, however, he covers his mouth while you are speaking, it is a sign that he feels *you* are lying! An unsettling sight for a public speaker to see is his audience all using this gesture while he's speaking. In a small audience or a one-to-one sales situation, it is wise to stop the presentation or delivery and ask, "Would you care to comment on what I've just said?" This allows the other person's objections to be brought out into the open, giving you the opportunity to qualify or clarify your statements and to answer questions.

Nose Touching

In essence, the nose-touch gesture is a sophisticated, disguised version of the mouth-guard gesture. It may consist of several light rubs below or on the side of the nose, or it may be one quick, almost undetectable touch.

One explanation of the origin of the nose-touch gesture is that, as the negative thought enters the mind, the subconscious instructs the hand to cover the mouth, but, at the last moment, in an attempt to appear less obvious, the hand pulls away from the mouth and a quick nose-touch gesture is the result. Another explanation is that nervousness from lying causes the delicate nerve endings in the nose to tingle, and the rubbing action takes place to satisfy this feeling. "But what if the person only has an itchy nose?" is frequently asked. A very deliberate rubbing or scratching action, as opposed to the light strokes of the nose-touch gesture, normally satisfies the itch in a person's nose. Like the mouth-guard gesture, it can be used both by the speaker to disguise his own deceit and by the listener who doubts the speaker's words.

The Eye Rub

'See no evil' reveals the wise monkey. The eye rub is the brain's attempt to block out the deceit, doubt or lie that it sees or to avoid having to look at the face of the person to whom he is telling the lie. Men, when lying, rub their eyes vigorously and if the lie is a big one, they will often look away towards the floor. Women use a small, gentle rubbing motion just below the eye, either because they have been brought up to avoid making robust gestures, or to avoid smudging their make-up. Untruthful women tend to avoid a listener's gaze by looking up at the ceiling.

'Lying through your teeth' is a common phrase referring to a gesture cluster of clenched teeth and a false smile, combined with an eye-rub and an averted gaze. Movie actors use this gesture to portray insincerity and hypocrisy.

The Ear Rub

This gesture is an attempt by the listener to 'hear no evil' as he tries to block the words by placing his hands around or over his ears. It is a sophisticated adult version of the hands-over-both-ears gesture used by the young child who wants to block out his parent's reprimands. Variations of the ear-rub gesture include rubbing the back of the ear, the finger drill (where the fingertip is screwed back and forth inside the ear), pulling at the earlobe or bending the entire ear forward to cover the ear hole. This last gesture is a signal that the person has heard enough and now wants to speak.

The Neck Scratch

In the neck scratch, the index finger of the writing hand scratches below the earlobe, or may even scratch the side of the neck. The person most often scratches five times. Rarely is the number of scratches less than five and seldom more than five. This gesture is a signal of doubt or uncertainty and is a nonverbal message meaning, "I'm not sure I agree." It is very noticeable when the verbal language contradicts it. For example, when the person says something such as, "I can understand how you feel," yet scratches his neck, one can be certain he is not in agreement with the speaker.

The Collar Pull

Desmond Morris noted that research into the gestures of those who tell lies revealed that the telling of a lie caused a tingling sensation in the delicate facial and neck tissues and a rub or scratch was required to satisfy it. This seems to be a reasonable explanation of why some people use the collar-pull gesture when they tell a lie and suspect that they have been caught. It's as if the lie causes a slight trickle of sweat to form on the neck of the deceiver when he feels that you believe he is lying. A person who is angry or frustrated often feels a need to pull his collar away from his neck in an attempt to let the cool air circulate around it. When talking with someone who is obsessively using this gesture, questions such as, "Would you repeat that, please?" or "Could you clarify that point, please?" could cause the would-be deceiver to give himself away.

Fingers in the Mouth

Usually fingers are placed in the mouth when a person is under pressure. It is a subconscious attempt by the person to revert to the security of his childhood as he sucked a bottle or his mother's breast. After a few years, the young child substitutes his thumb for the breast and as an adult he substitutes his fingers. Not only are fingers placed in the mouth but insecure adults also insert such things as pencils, pins, paper clips, pipes and the like into it. Whereas most hand-to-mouth gestures involve lying or deception, the fingers-in-mouth gesture is an outward manifestation of an inner need for reassurance. Giving guarantees and assurances is the appropriate response if you notice this gesture in another person.

Interpreting and Misinterpreting

The ability to accurately interpret hand-to-face gestures in a given set of circumstances takes considerable time and conscious observation to acquire. We can confidently assume that, when a person uses one of the hand-to-face gestures just described, a negative thought has entered his mind. The question is, "What is negative?" It could be doubt, deceit, uncertainty, exaggeration, apprehension or outright lying. The real skill of interpretation is the ability to pick which of the negatives mentioned is the correct one. This can best be done by an analysis of the gestures that precede the hand-to-face gesture and then interpreting it in context.

A friend of mine whom I play blackjack with often rubs his ear or touches his nose during the game, but only when he is unsure of his next move. I have discovered that when I signal the dealer my intention for another card, my friend immediately uses gesture clusters that signal what he thinks about my proposed hand. If he sits back in his chair and uses a steepling gesture (confidence), I can assume that he has anticipated my move and may already have

mistake, as the listener inevitably responds to this look with folded arms, crossed legs and a correspondingly negative attitude. People who wear reading glasses should remove them when speaking and put them back on to listen. This not only relaxes the other person but also allows the wearer to have control of the conversation. The listener quickly learns that when the glasses are off, he must not interrupt the speaker, and when they are put back on, he had better start talking.

Smoking Gestures

Smoking is an outward manifestation of an inner turmoil or conflict. It is one of the displacement activities that people in today's high-pressure society use to release the tensions that build up from social and business encounters.

Smoking gestures play an important part in assessing a person's attitude, as they are usually performed in a predictable, ritualistic manner. The cigarette ritual involving tapping, twisting, flicking, waving and other mini-gestures indicates that the person is experiencing more tension than may be normal.

The direction in which the smoke is exhaled, up or down, indicates whether the person has a positive or negative attitude towards his circumstances. A person who is feeling positive, superior or confident will blow the smoke in an upward direction most of the time. Conversely, a person in a negative, secretive or suspicious frame of mind will exhale cigarette smoke in a downward motion. Blowing cigarette smoke down and from the corner of the mouth indicates an even more negative or secretive attitude. There also appears to be a relationship between how positive or negative the person feels and the speed at which he or she exhales the smoke. The faster the smoke is blown upwards, the more superior or confident the person feels; the faster it is blown down, the more negative he feels.

Observation of smoking gestures during a sales encounter, shows that when a smoker is asked to buy, those who have reached a positive decision blow their cigarette smoke upwards, whereas those who have decided not to buy blow it downwards. To allow the customer time to reconsider his decision, the alert salesperson, seeing the smoke being blown downwards during the close of a sale should quickly resell the customer on all the benefits he would receive by purchasing the product. Blowing smoke out through the nostrils is a sign of a superior, confident individual who may be irritated and trying to look ferocious, like an angry bull.

.Pipe smokers perform a cleaning, lighting, tapping, filling, packing and puffing ritual with their pipes as a very useful way for them to relieve tension when they are under pressure. Sales research has shown that pipe smokers usually take longer to make a decision to buy than do cigarette smokers or non-smokers. The pipe ritual is usually performed during the tense moments of the sales presentation. Pipe smokers, it seems, are people who like to stall decision-making and do so in an unobtrusive and socially acceptable way.

Cigars have always been used as a means of displaying superiority because of their cost and size. Cigars are used to celebrate a victory or achievement such as the birth of a baby or clinching a business deal; therefore, it is not surprising that most of the smoke exhaled by cigar smokers is upwards.

The continual tapping of a cigar or cigarette end on an ashtray shows that the smoker is experiencing an inner conflict and that you may need to reassure him. Another interesting smoking phenomenon is that most smokers smoke their cigarette down to a certain length before extinguishing it in the ashtray. If the smoker lights a cigarette and suddenly extinguishes it earlier than he normally would, he has signaled his decision to terminate the conversation. Watching for this termination signal can allow you to take control and close the conversation, making it appear that it was your idea to end it.

Head-Rubbing and Head-Slapping Gestures

An exaggerated version of the collar-pull gesture is the palm rubbing the back of the neck in what is labeled as the 'pain-in-the-neck' gesture. It is a gesture often associated with frustration or anger and, when this is the case, the angry person slaps the back of his neck first and then begins to rub his neck. Let us assume, for example, that you asked a subordinate to complete a certain task for you and that the subordinate had forgotten to do it within the time required. When you ask him for the results, he nonverbally signals his forgetfulness by slapping his head, either on the forehead or the back of the neck, as if he were symbolically hitting himself. Although slapping of the head communicates forgetfulness, the person signals how he feels about you or the situation by the position where he slaps his hand on his head, either his forehead or his neck. If he slaps his forehead, he signals that he is not intimidated by your having mentioned his forgetfulness, but when he slaps the back of his neck, he is nonverbally telling you that you are literally a 'pain-in-the-neck' for pointing out his error. Those who habitually rub the backs of their necks have a tendency to be negative or critical of others, whereas those who routinely rub their foreheads to nonverbalize an error tend to be open, easy-going and critical of themselves.

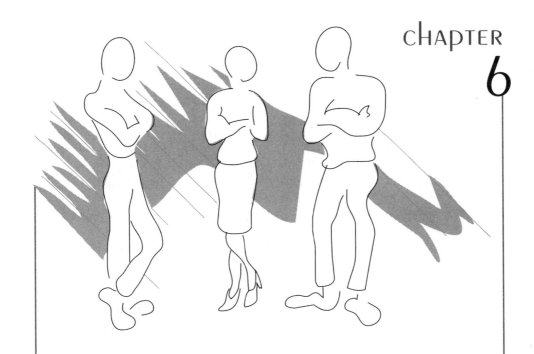

Nervous, Negative or Defensive: Arm Barriers

Hiding behind a barrier is a normal human response that is learned at an early age as a means of protection. As children, we hid behind solid objects such as tables, chairs, furniture and our mother's skirts whenever we found ourselves in a threatening situation. This hiding behavior becomes more sophisticated as we grow up, and by the age of six, when it is unacceptable to hide behind solid objects, we learn to fold our arms tightly across our chests whenever a threatening situation arises. During our teens, we learn to make this crossed-arms gesture a little less obvious by relaxing our arms and combining the gesture with crossed legs.

Folded-Arms Gestures

If you go into a client's office, and her arms are already crossed, notice the room temperature. She might just be cold! Or she may have just gotten off the phone from an unpleasant conversation. Maybe she's thinking about the argument she had with her spouse the previous night. The point is this: you can't attribute her gesture to your being there until she does something in reaction to something you do or say. Once you've started your presentation and she suddenly crosses her arms, then you can be fairly certain that you caused this reaction. Now is the time to stop what you're doing and find out why the client is reacting that way towards you.

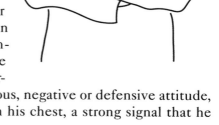

By folding one or both arms across the chest, a barrier is formed that is, in essence, an attempt to block out the impending threat or undesirable circumstances. One thing is certain; when a person has a nervous, negative or defensive attitude, he will fold his arms firmly on his chest, a strong signal that he feels threatened.

Research conducted about the folded-arms position in body language has shown some interesting results. When a listener folds his arms, not only has he negative thoughts about the speaker, but he is also paying less attention to what is being said. Because of this fact, it would be wise if training centers had chairs with arms to allow the attendees to leave their arms uncrossed and become more receptive to the seminar.

People claim that they habitually take the arms-folded position because it is comfortable. Any gesture will feel comfortable when you have the corresponding attitude; that is, if you have a negative, defensive or nervous attitude, the folded-arms position will feel good.

It is imperative to remember that in nonverbal communication, the meaning of the message is also in the receiver, not only the sender. You may feel 'comfortable' with your arms crossed or your back and neck stiffened, but studies have shown that the reception of these gestures is negative.

Standard Arm-Cross Gesture

In the standard arm-cross position, both arms are folded together across the chest as an attempt to 'hide' from an unfavorable situation. This universal gesture signifies the same defensive or negative attitude almost everywhere. It is commonly seen when a person is among strangers in public meetings, lines, cafeterias, elevators or anywhere that he feels uncertain or insecure. Experienced speakers know that this gesture demonstrates the necessity of a good 'ice breaker' to move an unreceptive audience into a more open posture that will alter their attitudes.

When you see the arm-cross gesture occur during a face-to-face encounter, it is reasonable to assume that you have said something with which the other person disagrees, so it is pointless to continue your line of argument even though the other person may be verbally agreeing with you. The nonverbal medium does not lie—the mouth lies. Your objective should be to try to discover the cause of the arms-folded gesture and to move the person into a more receptive position. Remember: as long as the arms-folded gesture remains, the negative attitude will remain. The attitude causes the gestures to occur and prolonging the gesture forces the attitude to remain.

A simple, but effective, method of breaking the folded-arms position is to hand the person a pen, a book or something that forces him to unfold his arms to reach forward. This moves him into a more open posture and accepting attitude. Asking the person to lean forward to look at a visual presentation can also be an effective means of opening the folded-arms position. Another useful method is to lean forward with your palms facing up and say, "I can see you have a question, what would you like to know?" or, "What do you think?" and then sit back to indicate that it is the other person's turn to speak or ask questions. By leaving your palms visible, you nonverbally tell the other person that you would like an open, honest answer. A salesperson should never proceed with the presentation of a product until he has uncovered the prospective buyer's reason for suddenly folding his arms.

Reinforced Arm-Cross

If as well as the bold arm-cross gesture the person has clenched fists, he is indicating to you that he has a hostile and defensive attitude. This cluster is often combined with clenched teeth and a red face, in which case a verbal or physical attack may be imminent. A submissive palms-up approach is needed to discover what caused the hostile gestures if the reason is not already apparent. The person using this gesture cluster has an attacking attitude, as opposed to the person using the standard arm-cross and is only taking on a defending position.

Arm-Gripping Gesture

Hands tightly gripping the upper arms to reinforce the position and to stop any attempt to unfold the arms and expose the body, characterize this arm-cross gesture. The arms can often be gripped so tightly that the fingers and knuckles turn white as the blood circulation is cut off. This arm-fold style is common to people sitting in a doctor or dentist's waiting room, or first time air travelers who are waiting for the plane to take off. It depicts a negative, restrained attitude.

Status can influence arm-folding gestures. A superior type can make his superiority felt in the presence of persons he has just met by the manner in which he holds or unfolds his arms. For example, at a company social function, the general manager is introduced to several new employees whom he has not met. Having greeted them with a dominant handshake, he stands at the social distance from the new employees with his hands by his sides, behind his back in the superior palm-in-palm position, or with one hand in his pocket. He rarely folds his arms to show the slightest hint of nervousness. Conversely, after shaking hands with the boss, the new employees take full or partial arm-fold gestures because of their apprehension about being in the presence of the company's top man. Both the general manager and the new employees feel comfortable with their respective gestures as each is signaling his status relative to the other. But what happens when the general manager meets a young, up-and-coming executive who is also a superior type and who may even feel that he is as important as the general manager? The likely outcome is that after the two have exchanged a dominant handshake, the young executive will make an arm-fold gesture across his body then leave both of his thumbs pointing vertically upwards. The thumbs-up gesture is a person's way of showing that he has a self-confident attitude and the folded arms give him a feeling of protection.

A salesperson, seeing the thumbs-up, needs to analyze why a buyer may have made this gesture to know whether his approach is effective. If the thumbs-up gesture has come towards the end of the sales presentation and is combined with many other positive gestures, the salesperson can move comfortably into closing the sale and should ask for the order. If, on the other hand, at the close of the sale, the buyer moves into the fists-clenched arm-cross position and has a poker face, the salesperson can be inviting disastrous consequences by attempting to ask for the order. Instead, he should quickly go back to his sales presentation and ask more questions to try to discover the buyer's objection. In selling, once the buyer verbalizes, "No," it can become difficult to change his decision. The ability to read and accurately interpret body language allows you to see the negative decision before it is verbalized and gives you time to take an alternative course of action.

Partial Arm-Cross Barriers

The full arm-cross gesture is sometimes too obvious to use around others because it tells them that we are negative or fearful. Occasionally, we substitute a subtler version—the partial arm-cross, in which one arm swings across the body to hold or touch the other arm to form the barrier.

The partial arm barrier is often seen at meetings where one person is a stranger to the group or is lacking in self-confidence. Another popular version of a partial arm barrier is when a person holds hands with his own self, a gesture commonly used by a person who must stand before a crowd to receive an award or give a speech. Desmond Morris found that this gesture allowed a person to relive the emotional security he experienced as a child when his parent held his hand under fearful circumstances.

Disguised Arm-Cross Gestures

Disguised arm-cross gestures are highly sophisticated gestures used by people who are continually exposed to others. This group includes politicians, salespeople, television personalities and the like who do not want their audience to detect that they are unsure of themselves or nervous. Like all arm-cross gestures, one arm swings across in front of the body to grasp the other arm but instead of the arms folding, one hand touches a handbag, bracelet, watch, shirt cuff or other object on or near the other arm. Once again the barrier is formed and the secure feeling is achieved. When cufflinks were popular, men constantly adjusted them as they crossed a room or dance floor where they were in full view of others. A man may simply adjust the band on his watch, check the contents of his wallet, clasp or rub his hands together, play with a button on his cuff or use any other gesture that allows his arms to cross in front of his body in an effort to help him feel secure. To the trained observer, however, these gestures are a dead giveaway because they achieve no real purpose except as an attempt to disguise nervousness.

Women are less obvious than men in their use of disguised arm-barrier gestures. They can grasp such things as handbags or books when they become unsure of themselves and no one thinks much of it. One common version of this is when a woman holds a glass of wine or soft drink with both hands. Did it ever occur to you that you need only one hand to hold a glass of wine? The use of two hands to hold the drink allows the nervous person to form an almost undetectable arm barrier.

Reassuring the Nervous Customer

Your relaxed and open postures will do wonders in reducing your prospect's initial apprehension. Some clients are harder to 'open up' than others. They may feel insecure or frustrated or they may be bored or overworked in their jobs. These complicated feelings show up as disinterest, hostility or simply nervousness. Some helpful hints for relaxing this type of client can be gained from one profession that must constantly sell 'unwanted' services—dentistry.

Dentists and their staffs are aware of the anxiety their services produce. They also realize that those who say they're not nervous may be the jitteriest patrons, so they look for 'displacement gestures.' Tapping fingers, flipping through magazines aimlessly, fiddling with objects and chain-smoking all indicate nervous energy. To calm their patients, dentists know that they need to reassure them through pleasant music, calm conversation and light humor. They know that their main goal is to assure the patient, through their own actions, that everything is fine.

In selling, you may notice similar displacement gestures. To help calm such a prospect, remember to:

1. Avoid 'mirroring' the client's negative nonverbal gestures or movements. Resist the subtle, subconscious urge to respond to these gestures by scratching your head, fiddling with a pen, jiggling coins in your pocket or by shifting your posture too often.
2. Lead the client to imitate your own expressions of confidence and reassurance. Communicate relaxed gestures and postures. Maintain a comfortable distance between yourself and your client and consciously lower your shoulders (raised shoulders indicate tension) and slightly tilt your head (shows interest).

Sales Hype
OR
Selling Strategy:
Leg Barriers

Most people believe that leg crossing is done for comfort. Did you ever stop to think *why* people are comfortable in that position? Usually it's because their bodies are reflecting how they feel inside. A study of 2,000 people found that *no* sales were made while participants had their legs crossed. Even if all other channels appear to be open and positive, the customer who crosses his legs may have some minor reservations that will prevent you from completing the sale if they are not uncovered and answered.

During a sales call much of the time is spent sitting down. That's why it is worth your time to develop and practice a comfortable, positive sitting position.

Study yourself when you walk into a room and sit down, what do you automatically do with your body? Scan your five nonverbal channels to check for signals that are detrimental in a sales situation. Do you lean back in your chair? Are your hands folded tightly, tucked under your arms in fists or grasping the arms of the chair? Do you cross your legs, tuck them under the chair, stick them way out in front of you or cross them at the ankles?

Experiment until you find an open, relaxed position that you can use *all the time*. Next, constantly be aware of how you sit, every time you sit. Shift into your new comfortable position whenever you fall back into your old habits. With practice, your new position will become your automatic one.

CROSSED-LEG GESTURES

Like arm-barrier gestures, crossed legs signal that a negative or defensive attitude exists. The purpose of crossing the arms on the chest was originally to defend the heart and upper body region. Crossing the legs is an attempt to shield and protect the genital area. Crossed arms indicate a more negative attitude than crossed legs do, and the crossed-arms gesture is more obvious than the crossed-legs gesture. Care should be taken when interpreting crossed-leg gestures on women as many are taught that this is how to 'sit like a lady.' Unfortunately for them, however, the gesture can make women appear defensive.

Two basic male crossed-leg sitting positions exist, the standard leg cross and the leg lock in the shape of the number four cross.

The European Leg-Cross Position

One leg is crossed neatly over the other, usually the right over the left. This is the normal male crossed-leg position seen in European cultures and typically displays a nervous, reserved or defensive attitude. However, this position is frequently a supportive gesture that occurs with other negative gestures and should not be interpreted in isolation or out of context. For example, people often sit this way during lectures or if they are in uncomfortable chairs for long periods. It is also common to see this gesture in cold weather. When the crossed-legs gesture is combined with crossed arms, the person has withdrawn from the conversation. A salesperson would be very foolish even to attempt to ask for a decision from a buyer if the buyer has taken this pose. A wise salesperson would ask probing questions to uncover the buyer's objection. The crossed-arms, crossed-legs pose is also popular among women who want to show their displeasure with a mate.

The Leg-Lock Position

The leg lock in the shape of the number four sitting position indicates that an argumentative or competitive attitude exists. It is the pose used by many American males who are locked into their own ideas.

In a selling situation, it would be unwise to attempt to close the sale and ask for the order when the buyer takes this position. The salesperson would need to use an open appeal, lean forward with his palms up and say, "I can see you have some ideas on this. I'd be interested in your opinion," and then sit back to signify that it is the buyer's turn to speak. This gives the buyer an opportunity to tell you his opinion. Women wearing trousers or jeans are often observed sitting in this leg-lock position when they are opposed to another person's ideas.

Leg Clamp and the Leg Lock

The person who has a hard and fast attitude in an argument or debate will often lock the leg into place with one or both hands, using them as a clamp. This is a sign of the tough minded, stubborn individual who may need a special approach to break through his resistance.

Standing Leg-Cross Gestures

The next time you attend a meeting or function, you will notice small groups of people all standing with their arms and legs crossed. Further observation will reveal that they are standing at a greater distance from each other than is customary, and that, if they are wearing coats or jackets, they are usually buttoned. If you were to question these people, you would find that one or all of them are strangers to the others in the group. Most people stand this way when they are among people whom they do not know well.

Now you notice another small group in which the people are standing with their arms unfolded, palms exposed, coats unbuttoned, leaning on one foot with their other foot pointing towards the other members of the group and moving in and out of each other's intimate zones. Close investigation reveals that these people are friends or personally know each other. Interestingly, the people using the closed arms and legs stance may have relaxed facial expressions and conversation that sounds free and easy, but the folded arms and legs tell you that they are not relaxed or confident.

The next time you join a group of people who are standing in the open friendly stance but among whom you know no one, stand with your arms and legs tightly crossed. One by one the group members will cross their arms and legs and remain in that position until you leave them. Then walk away and watch how, one by one, the members of the group assume their original open pose once again!

The 'Opening-Up' Procedure

As people begin to feel comfortable in a group and get to know others in it, they move through an unwritten code of movements taking them from the defensive crossed arms and legs position to a relaxed open position.

Step 1: Defensive position, arms and legs are crossed.

Step 2: Legs are uncrossed and feet are placed together in a neutral position.

Step 3: The arm folded on top in the arm-cross comes out and the palm is flashed while the person is speaking. It is not tucked back into the arm-cross position; instead the speaker uses it to hold the outside of his other arm.

Step 4: Arms unfold. The speaker gesticulates with one arm then places it on his hip or in his pocket.

Step 5: As interest develops, a person leans back on one leg and pushes his other leg forward to point at the person he finds the most appealing.

Defensive or Cold?

Many people claim that they are not defensive but cross their arms or legs because they feel cold. This is a cover-up. Note the difference between a defensive stance and the way a person stands when he or she feels cold. First of all, when someone wants to warm his hands he normally thrusts them under his armpits rather than tucking them under his elbows, as is the case with a defensive arm-cross. Secondly, when a person feels cold he will fold his arms in a type of body hug. His crossed legs are usually straight, stiff and pressed hard against each other, as opposed to the more relaxed leg posture of the defensive stance or position.

People who habitually take a crossed arms or legs position prefer to say that they are cold or comfortable rather than to admit that they could be nervous, shy or defensive.

The Ankle-Lock Gesture

Just as the crossed or folded arms or legs suggest a negative or defensive attitude, it is also the case with the ankle-lock gesture. The male version of the ankle lock is often combined with clenched fists resting on the knees or with the hands tightly gripping the arms of the chair. The female version varies slightly; the knees are held together, the feet are to one side and the hands relax side by side or one on top of the other on the upper legs.

During interviews or sales presentations, it is noted that the interviewee who locks his ankles is mentally 'biting his lip.' The locked-ankle gesture represents someone who is holding back a negative attitude, emotion, nervousness or fear. If the interviewer tries walking around to the job applicant's side of the desk and sits beside him, removing the desk barrier, the job applicant's ankles usually unlock and the conversation takes on an open, more personal atmosphere.

Leaders in the field of negotiating techniques find that whenever one party locks his ankles during a negotiation it means that he is holding back a valuable concession. They found that, by using proper questioning techniques and positive nonverbal communication, they could often encourage the other party to unlock his ankles and reveal his hidden fears.

There are always people who claim that they habitually sit in the ankle-lock position, or for that matter, any of the negative arm and leg clusters, because they feel comfortable. If you are one of these people, remember that any arm or leg position will feel comfortable when you have a defensive, negative or reserved attitude. Considering that a negative gesture can increase or prolong a negative attitude, and that other people interpret you as being defensive or negative, you would be well advised to practice using positive and open gestures to improve your self-confidence and relationships with others.

When analyzing leg crosses, take female fashion trends into consideration. Particularly notice how a woman's clothing might affect her leg positions, before jumping to conclusions.

The Foot Lock

Women who are shy or timid commonly use this gesture. The top of one foot locks around the other leg to reinforce a defensive attitude. When this gesture appears, you can be sure that the woman has become a mental recluse or has retreated like a tortoise into her shell. A warm, friendly, low-key approach is needed if you eventually hope to open this clam.

Other Typical Leg Positions

Feet on desk: this position indicates an attitude of ownership, superiority and dominance. It is not a posture that will elicit cooperation from the client. Instead, it says "Go ahead and try to sell me."

Legs crossed away from: this nonverbal gesture tells you that the sales call is not going well. When legs are in this position, the body is also shifted away from the other person. Cross your legs toward your client, if you must cross them at all.

Uncrossed: this is the ideal position for both you and your client. It sends a message of cooperation, confidence and friendly interest in the other person. Use it as much as possible!

Legs crossed toward: to encourage your client to assume an open posture, this position is acceptable in the early phase of a sale. Mirroring your client's position in this situation may make him feel that the two of you are alike and tuned in to each other.

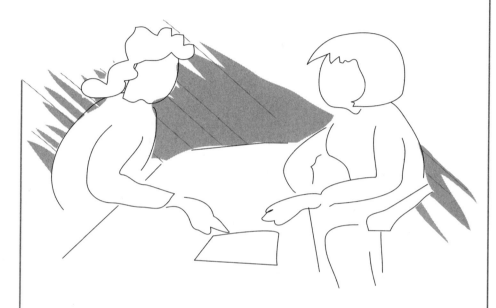

Anatomy of an Encounter:
Eye Signals and Other
Popular Gestures
and Actions

At the point of entering a crowded room you pause for a moment by the door and search for someone with a familiar face. You see a casual acquaintance, catch his eye and walk towards him. Greetings are exchanged; you shake hands, chat for a while, and then move away to talk with somebody else.

During every encounter, however brief, hundreds of nonverbal messages are exchanged. It's these cues, usually more than any words spoken, that influence the impression you form on one another.

Eye Signals

Body language specialists have been preoccupied with the eye and its effect on human behavior. We've all used such phrases as "He has shifty eyes," "She gave me the evil eye," or "He had that gleam in his eye." When we use these phrases, we unwittingly refer to the size of the person's pupils and to his or her gaze behavior. Eyes may well be the most revealing and accurate of all human communication signals because they are a focal point on the body and work independently of all other body parts.

In given light conditions, a person's pupils will dilate or contract as his attitude and mood changes from positive to negative and vice versa. When someone becomes excited, his pupils can dilate up to four times their normal size. Conversely, an angry or negative mood causes an individual's pupils to contract. This narrowing of a person's pupils is commonly referred to as 'beady eyes' or 'snake eyes.'

Once eye contact is made with another person, each individual scans the other's face for further information about attitudes and intentions based on silent speech signals.

Tests conducted with expert card players show that fewer games were won by the experts when their opponents wore dark glasses. If an opponent were dealt four aces in a game of poker and his eyes were visible, the expert would unconsciously detect his rapid pupil dilation. Knowing this, the expert would definitely not raise his bet.

The ancient Chinese gem traders watched the pupil dilation of their buyers when negotiating prices. The late Aristotle Onassis was noted for wearing dark glasses when discussing business deals so that his eyes would not reveal his thoughts.

The old cliché says, "Look a person in the eye when you talk to him." While communicating or negotiating with others, practice 'looking them in the pupil' and you'll get insight into their true feelings.

Gaze Behavior

A genuine basis for communication is established when you can see 'eye to eye' with another person. While some people can make us feel quite comfortable when they converse with us, others can make us feel ill at ease. This has to do primarily with the length of time they look at us or hold our gaze as they speak to us. When a person is being dishonest or holding back information, his eyes meet ours less than one-third of the time. When a person's gaze meets yours for more than two-thirds of the time, it can mean one of two things; first, he or she finds you very interesting or appealing, in which case, the gaze will be associated with dilated pupils; secondly, he or she is hostile towards you and may be issuing a nonverbal challenge; in this case, the pupils constrict. In studying eye gaze, it has been reported that when person A likes person B, he will look at him a lot. This causes B to think that A likes him, so B will like A in return. In other words, to build a good rapport with another person, your gaze should meet his about 60 to 70 percent of the time. This will also make him begin to like you. It is not surprising, therefore, that the nervous, timid person who meets your gaze less than one-third of the time is rarely trusted. Dark tinted glasses should be avoided during negotiations because proper eye contact cannot be established. The dark glasses make others feel that you are staring at them or that you have something to hide.

The length of time that one person gazes at another is culturally determined. Southern Europeans have such a high frequency of gaze that it is sometimes offensive to others and the Japanese gaze at the neck rather than at the face when conversing. Always be sure to consider cultural circumstances before jumping to conclusions.

Not only is the length of your gaze significant, just as important is the geographical area of the person's face and body at which you direct your gaze, as this also affects the outcome of a negotiation. These gaze signals are transmitted and received nonverbally and are accurately interpreted by the receiver.

The Business Gaze

During discussions on a business level, imagine that there is a triangle on the other person's forehead. By keeping your gaze directed at this area, between the other person's eyes and up to his forehead, you create a serious atmosphere and the other person senses that you mean business. Provided that your gaze does not drop below the level of the other person's eyes, you are usually able to maintain control of the interaction.

The Social Gaze

When your gaze drops below the other person's eye level, a social atmosphere develops. During social encounters, the gazer's eyes also look in a triangular area on the other person's face, in this case, between the eyes and the mouth.

The Intimate Gaze

This gaze goes across the eyes and below the chin to other parts of the person's body. In close encounters it is the triangular area between the eyes and the chest or breasts. Men and women use this gaze to show interest in each other.

Sideways Glance

The sideways glance is used to communicate either interest or hostility. When it is combined with slightly raised eyebrows or a smile, it communicates interest and is frequently used as a courtship signal. If it is combined with down-turned eyebrows, furrowed brow or the corners of the mouth down-turned, it signals a suspicious, hostile or critical attitude.

Eye-Block Gesture

Some of the most irritating people with whom we deal are those who use the eye-block gesture as they speak. This gesture occurs unconsciously and is an attempt by the person to block you from his sight because he has become bored or uninterested in you and feels that he is superior to you. Compared to the normal rate of six to eight blinks per minute during a conversation, during the eye-block gesture the eyelids close and remain closed for a second or longer as the person momentarily wipes you from his mind. The ultimate blockout is to leave the eyes closed and to fall asleep; hopefully this rarely happens during one-to-one encounters.

If a person feels superior to you, he uses the eye-block gesture and tilts his head backwards to give you a long look. It is commonly known as 'looking down one's nose' at someone else. When you see an eye-block gesture during a conversation, it is a signal that the approach you are using may be causing a negative reaction and that a new tack is needed if effective communication is to take place.

Controlling a Person's Gaze

When you are giving another person a visual presentation using books, charts or graphs, it is wise to gain control of his visual gaze. Research shows that of the information relayed to a person's brain, 55 percent comes via the eyes, 38 percent via the ears and 7 percent via the other senses. To maintain maximum control of another

person's gaze, use a pen or pointer to point to the visual aid, while at the same time, verbalize what he sees. Next, lift the pen from the visual aid and hold it between his eyes and your own eyes. This movement has the magnetic effect of making him lift his head so that he is now looking at your eyes and sees and hears more clearly what you are saying. He is achieving maximum absorption of your message. Be sure that the palm of your other hand (open gesture) is visible when you are speaking.

Head Gestures

The two most widely used head movements are the head nod and the head shake. The head nod is a positive gesture used in most cultures to signify 'yes,' or affirmation. Research conducted with people who have been deaf and blind from birth shows that they also use this gesture to signify affirmation, which has given rise to the theory that this is an inborn gesture. The head shake, usually meaning 'no,' is also claimed to be an inborn action. It is, in fact, the first gesture a human being learns. When the newborn baby has had enough milk, he shakes his head from side to side to reject his bottle or his mother's breast. Similarly, the young child who has had enough to eat uses the head shake to reject his parent's attempt to spoon feed him.

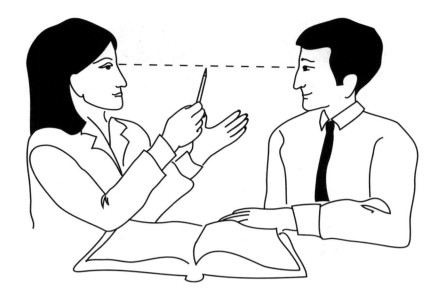

The easiest way to uncover a disguised objection when dealing with others is to watch if the person uses the head shake gesture while verbalizing his agreement with you. Take, for example, the person who verbalizes, "Yes, I can see your point of view," while shaking his head from side to side. Even though his words may sound convincing, his head shake gesture signals that a negative attitude exists and you would be well advised to reject what he has said and to question him further.

Basic Head Positions

There are three basic head positions. The first is the head up position and is taken by someone who has a neutral attitude about what he is hearing. The head remains still and may occasionally give small nods. Hand-to-cheek evaluation gestures are often used with this position.

When the head tilts to one side, it shows that interest has developed. Charles Darwin was the first to note that humans, as well as animals, tilt their heads to one side when they become interested in something. If you are giving a sales presentation or delivering a speech, always make a point of looking for this gesture in your audience. When you notice them tilt their heads and lean

forward using hand-to-chin evaluation gestures, you are getting your point across. When someone is speaking to you, use the head-tilted position and head nods to make him understand that you are listening to him.

When the head is down, it signals that the attitude is negative and even judgmental or critical. Unless you can get the person's head up or tilted, you may have a communication problem. Professional speakers and trainers usually do something that involves audience participation before they begin to address a group. This is intended to get the audience's heads up and to get their attention.

Both Hands Behind Head

This gesture is typical of a professional who is feeling confident, dominant or superior. It is as if he is saying, "I have all the answers," or "Everything's under control." It is a gesture used by the 'know-it-all' individual and most people find it irritating when someone does it to them. It is often used as a territorial sign to show that a person has staked a claim to a particular area.

There are several ways to handle this gesture, depending on the circumstances in which it occurs. If you want to discover the reason for the person's superior attitude, lean forward with palms up and say, "I can see that you know about this. Would you care to comment?" Then sit back, palms still visible, and wait for an answer. Another method is to force the person to change his position, which will in turn change his attitude. This can be accomplished by placing something just out of his reach and asking, "Have you seen this?" It forces the other person to release his hand clasp and lean forward. Copying the gesture is another good way to handle it.

On the other hand, if the person using the hands-behind-head gesture is reprimanding you, you will nonverbally intimidate him by copying his gesture. For example, two lawyers will use this gesture in each other's presence to show equality and agreement, but the mischievous schoolboy would infuriate the school principal if he used it in the principal's office.

The origin of this gesture is uncertain, but it is likely that the hands are used as an imaginary armchair in which the person lies back and relaxes.

Straddling a Chair

Centuries ago, men used shields to protect themselves from the spears and clubs of the enemy, and today, civilized man uses whatever he has at his disposal to symbolize this same protective behavior when he is under physical or verbal attack. This includes standing behind a gate, doorway, desk, the open door of his motor vehicle and straddling a chair. The back of the chair provides a shield to protect his body and transforms him into an aggressive, dominant warrior. Most chair straddlers slip into the straddle position unnoticed. They are discreet and overbearing individuals who will try to take control of other people or groups when they become bored with the conversation. The back of the chair serves as good protection from any 'attack' by other members of the group.

The easiest way to disarm the straddler is to stand or sit behind him, making him feel vulnerable to attack and forcing him to change his position, becoming less aggressive. With his back exposed, it makes him feel uncomfortable and unprotected.

How do you handle a one-to-one confrontation with a straddler on a swivel chair? It is pointless to try to reason with him, particularly when he is on a swiveling merry-go-round, so the best defense is a nonverbal attack. Conduct your conversation standing above and looking down upon him. Try moving within his personal territory. This invasion is very disconcerting to him and he may even fall backwards off his chair in an attempt to avoid being forced to change position.

If you have a straddler coming to visit you and his aggressive attitude annoys you, be sure to seat him on a fixed chair with arms to stop him from taking his favorite position.

Picking Imaginary Lint

When a person disapproves of the opinions or attitudes of others but feels inhibited in giving his point of view, he performs displacement nonverbal gestures. Picking imaginary pieces of lint from his own clothing is one such gesture. The lint-picker usually looks away from the other people or towards the floor while performing this minor, irrelevant action. He is signaling disapproval. When the listener continually picks imaginary pieces of lint off his clothing it is a good indication that he does not like what is being said, even though he may be verbally agreeing with everything.

Open your palms and say, "Well, what do you think?" or, "I can see that you have some thoughts on this. Would you mind telling me what they are?" Sit back, arms apart, palms visible and wait for an answer. If the person says he is in agreement with you but continues to pick the imaginary lint, you may need to take an even more direct approach to discover his hidden objection.

Aggressive and Readiness Gestures

The most common gesture used by man to communicate an uncompromising attitude is the hands-on-hips pose. It is a readiness gesture that carries with it an aggressive meaning. It is called the achiever stance, describing the goal-directed individual who uses this position when he is ready to tackle his objectives. People use this gesture to show an argumentative, dominant attitude and to let others know that they're ready for action.

Birds fluff their feathers to make themselves appear bigger when they are fighting or courting; humans use the hands-on-hips gesture for the same purpose, that is, to make themselves appear larger and more threatening. Males will commonly use it as a non-verbal challenge to other males who enter their territory.

It is important to consider the circumstances and gestures immediately preceding the hands-on-hips pose to make a correct assessment of the person's attitude. Several other gestures can further support your conclusions. For example, is the coat open and pushed back on to the hips, or is it buttoned when this aggressive pose is taken? Closed-coat readiness shows aggressive frustration, whereas, when the coat is open and pushed back, it is a directly aggressive pose. The person is openly exposing his heart and throat in a nonverbal display of fearlessness. This position is further reinforced when the individual places his feet evenly apart on the ground or clenches his fists. Women use the aggressive-readiness hands-on-hips cluster gestures to display critical evaluation and an impatient attitude.

Seated Readiness

One of the most valuable gestures that a negotiator can learn to recognize is seated readiness, that is, when the buyer leans casually forward. In the selling situation, if the potential buyer were to take this gesture at the end of the sales presentation and the meeting had progressed successfully up to that point, the salesperson could ask for the order and expect to get it.

Video replays of insurance salespeople interviewing potential buyers revealed that, whenever the seated-readiness gesture followed the chin-stroking gesture, the client bought the policy. In contrast to this, if, during the close of the sale, the client took the arms-crossed position immediately following the chin-stroking gesture, the sale was usually unsuccessful. Unfortunately, most sales courses teach salespeople always to ask for the order with little regard for the client's body position and gestures. Learning to recognize such gestures as openness and readiness not only helps make more sales but helps to keep many more people in the selling profession.

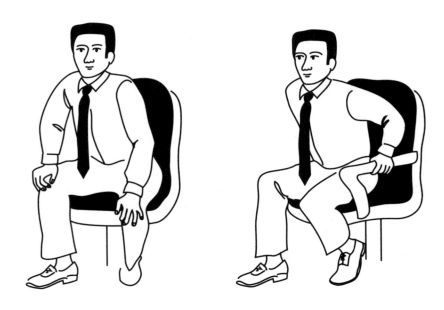

The Starter's Position

When a person leans forward in his chair and places both of his hands on both of his knees, or leans forward with both hands gripping his chair, he is signaling a desire to end a conversation or encounter. Should either of these occur in the middle of a conversation it would be wise for you to take the lead and terminate it. This allows you to maintain a psychological advantage in the negotiation and to keep the control.

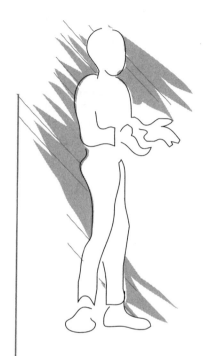

People Like People Who Are Like Themselves: Mirroring, Matching and Pointing

The next time you attend a social function or go to a place where people meet and interact, take note of the number of people who have adopted the identical gestures and posture of the person with whom they are talking. This 'mirroring' is a means by which one person tells the other that he is in agreement with his ideas and attitudes. In mirroring, you are nonverbally telling another person, "As you can see, I think the same as you, therefore I will copy your posture and gestures."

This copying of gestures occurs among people at the same status level or between good friends. It is common to see married couples walk, stand, sit and move in identical ways. Mirroring is one of the most important nonverbal lessons we can learn, for this is one way that others tell us that they agree with us or like us. It is also a way for us to tell others that we like them, by simply copying their gestures.

If an employer wishes to develop an immediate rapport and create a relaxed atmosphere with an employee, he need only copy the employee's posture to achieve this end. Similarly, an up-and-coming employee is often seen copying his boss's gestures in an attempt to show agreement. It is possible to influence a face-to-face encounter by copying the positive gestures and postures of the

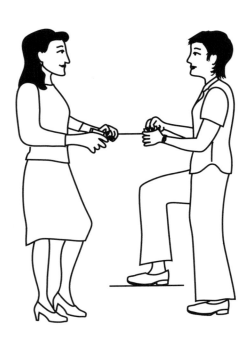

other person. It puts the other person in a receptive and relaxed frame of mind, as he can 'see' that you understand his point of view.

When meeting a 'cold' prospective customer, it is wise to deliberately copy the customer's positive movements until you feel that you have established a strong enough rapport to allow the presentation to proceed. Invariably, if the prospect begins to copy your gestures, a sale will typically result.

Research shows that when the leader of a group uses certain gestures and positions, subordinates copy them. Leaders tend to be the first of a group to walk through a doorway and typically prefer to sit on the end of a couch or bench rather than in the center of it. In the boardroom, the boss usually sits at the head of the table, often farthest from the door, and if he sits back in his chair and locks his hands behind his head, his subordinates will usually copy his position.

People who sell to married couples in their homes are well advised to watch the couple's gestures, to see who initiates the gestures and who follows.

For example, if the husband is doing all the talking and the wife sits there saying nothing, but you notice that the husband copies his wife's gestures, you will inevitably find that she makes the decisions and writes the check, so it is a good idea to direct your presentation to her.

Match Your Prospect's Language

You can get clues about the type of information your clients want to hear by listening to their own choice of words. Most people lean toward one of three major modes when communicating.

1. Visual-oriented language.
2. Auditory-oriented language.
3. Action-oriented language.

The clues they give you in their questions actually tell you how to phrase your statements and questions to get their attention.

Visual: Prospects who prefer visual information will use phrases such as, "That's *clear*," "I *see* what you mean," "Can you *show* that to me?" or "Can you *look* into that?" Charts, brochures and actually seeing the product will gain the interest of these clients. During your needs analysis and presentation, begin using phrases similar to the ones that your client uses. Also, make a mental note of the areas of your talk that you can stress to make the most of the client's visual preference.

AUDITORY: Customers who prefer auditory information use sound words such as "That *rings* a bell." "That doesn't *sound* quite right," "I don't think we're in *harmony* on this issue," or "They'll sure get a *bang* out of that." Anything that makes noise will interest this client—the pleasant click of a new machine, the soft chirping of modern telephone equipment, the quiet hum of a new computer. Also, these clients will be more attuned to your tone of voice, so concentrate on moderating your volume and using a good range of pitch. Make sure to include 'sound' words in your own vocabulary.

ACTION: Clients who desire action information use physical phrases such as "We'll have to *kick* that idea around," "I don't *grasp* what you are saying," "That doesn't *feel* right to me," or "We could use a *shot* in the arm." These are the people who love demonstrations where they can try out a product—they want to touch it, do it and hold onto it. Emphasize action words in your speech and zero in on anything in your presentation that moves.

Pointing

Have you ever had the feeling that someone to whom you are talking would rather be somewhere else than with you, even though he or she seems to be enjoying your company? A still photograph of that scene would probably reveal the following:

1. The person's head is turned *towards* you and facial signals such as smiling and nodding are evident.
2. The person's body and feet are pointing *away* from you, either towards another person or towards an exit.

The direction in which a person points his torso or feet is a signal of where he would prefer to be going.

During negotiations, when one person has decided to terminate the negotiation or wants to leave, he will turn his body or swing his feet to point towards the nearest exit. If you see these signals during a face-to-face encounter, you should do something to get the person involved and interested or else terminate the conversation on your terms, which allows you to maintain control in the situation.

Angles and Triangles: Open Formation

The angle at which people orient their bodies gives nonverbal clues to their attitudes and relationships with others. People in most English-speaking countries stand with their bodies oriented to form an angle of 90 degrees during ordinary social meetings. This serves as a nonverbal invitation for a third person to join in the conversation. The formation of the triangle invites a third person of similar status to join the conversation. When a fourth person is accepted into the group, a square will be formed and for a fifth person, either a circle is formed or two triangles are formed.

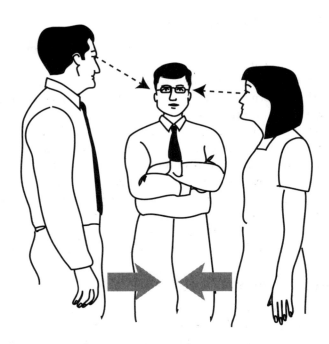

Angles and Triangles: Closed Formation

When intimacy or privacy is required by two people, the angle formed by their torsos decreases from 90 degrees down to 0 degrees. A man wishing to attract a female partner uses this ploy, as well as other courtship gestures, when he makes his play for her. Not only does he point his body towards her, but he also closes the distance between them as he moves into her intimate zone. To accept his approach, she need only orient her torso angle to 0 degrees and allow him to enter her territory. The distance between two people standing in the closed formation is usually less than that of people standing in the open formation.

Inclusion and Exclusion Techniques

Both the open triangular position and the closed position are used to include or exclude another person from the conversation.

When a third person wishes to join two others who are standing in a closed formation, he may be invited to join the conversation only when the other two orient their torsos towards a mutual third point to form a triangle. If the third person is not accepted, the others will hold the closed formation position and turn only their heads towards him as a sign of recognition but the direction of their torsos shows that he is not invited to remain.

Sometimes a conversation among three people begins in the open triangular formation, but eventually two take the closed formation to exclude the third person and give a clear signal to the third person that he should leave the group to avoid embarrassment.

Interviewing Two People

Let's assume that you, person C, are going to interview or talk to persons A and B, and let us say that by either choice or circumstance you are sitting in a triangular position at a round table. Let

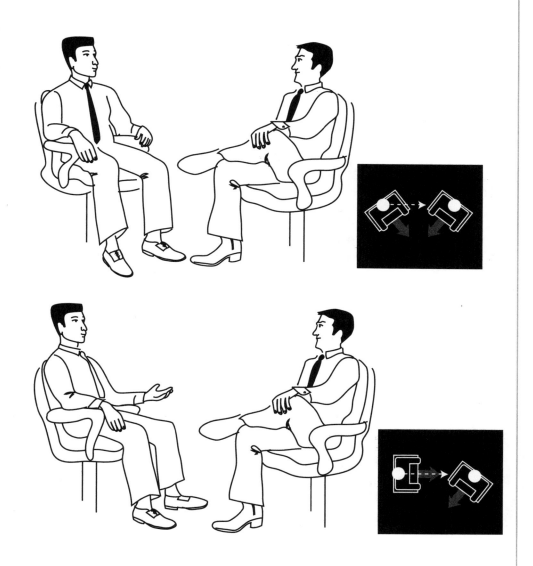

us also assume that person A is very talkative and asks many questions and that person B remains silent throughout. When A asks you a question, how can you answer him and carry on a conversation without making B feel excluded? Use this simple but highly effective inclusion technique: when A asks a question, look at him as you begin to answer, then turn your head towards B, then back to A, then to B again until you make your final statement, looking at A (who asked the question) again as you finish your sentence.

This technique lets B feel involved in the conversation and is particularly useful if you need to have B on your side.

Foot Pointing

Not only does a person's feet serve as pointers, indicating the direction in which he would like to go, but they are also used to point at people whom he finds interesting or attractive. Imagine that you are at a social function and you notice a group of three men and one attractive woman congregated together. The conversation seems to be dominated by the men and the woman is just listening. Upon further observation you notice that each man has one foot pointing towards the woman. With this simple nonverbal clue, the men are all telling the woman that they are interested in her. Subconsciously, the woman sees the foot gestures and is likely to remain with the group for as long as she is receiving this attention. She may eventually point one of her feet toward the man whom she finds the most appealing or intriguing.

Seated-Body Formations

If you are in a supervisory capacity and must counsel a subordinate whose work performance has been unsatisfactory and erratic, use the following body formations to nonverbally convey your message.

1. The fact that the counseling session is in your office and that you are the boss allows you to move from behind your desk to the employee's side (a cooperative position) and still maintain unspoken control.
2. The subordinate should be seated on a chair with fixed legs and no arms; one that forces him to use body gestures and postures, thus giving you a better understanding of his underlying attitude.
3. Sit on a swivel chair that has arms on it. This gives you more control and lets you eliminate or hide some of your own giveaway nervous gestures.

There are three main angle seated formations that can be used. Like the standing triangular position, the open triangular formation lends itself toward an informal, relaxed meeting and is a good position in which to open a counseling session. You can show nonverbal agreement with the subordinate from this position by copying his positive movements and gestures. As they do in the stand-

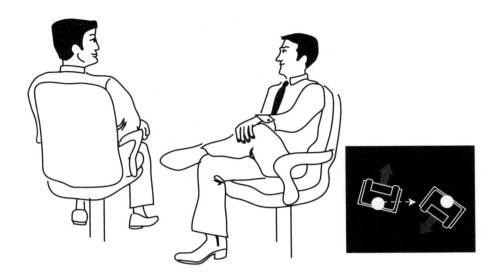

ing position, both torsos in the seated formation point to a third mutual point to form a triangle to show shared agreement.

By turning your chair to point your body directly at your subordinate, you are nonverbally telling him that you want direct answers to your questions. Combine this position with the business gaze and reduced body and facial gestures and your subject will feel tremendous nonverbal pressure. If, for example, after you have asked him a question, he rubs his eye and mouth and looks away when he answers, swing your chair to point directly at him and say, "Are you sure about that?" This simple movement exerts nonverbal pressure on him and can force him to tell the truth.

When you position your body at a right angle away from your subject, you take the pressure off the interview. It is an excellent position from which to ask delicate or embarrassing questions, encouraging more answers without any pressure coming from you. If the person you are trying to crack is a difficult one, you may need to revert to the direct body point technique to get to the facts.

Summary

If you want to build rapport with another person, use the triangular position and, when you need to exert nonverbal pressure, use the direct body point. The right angle position allows the other person to think and act independently, without nonverbal pressure from you.

These techniques take much practice to master but they can become 'natural' movements before long. If you deal with others for a living, mastery of body point and swivel chair techniques are useful skills to acquire. In your day-to-day encounters with others, proper use of foot pointing, body pointing and positive gesture clusters such as open arms, visible palms, leaning forward, head tilting and smiling can make it easy for others not only to enjoy your company, but also to be influenced by your point of view.

Power Plays: Strategic Office Layout—Desks, Chairs, and Seating Arrangements

Strategic positioning in relation to other people is an effective way to obtain cooperation from them. Aspects of their attitudes toward you can be revealed in the position they take in relation to you.

Although there is a general formula for interpretation of seating positions, the environment may have an effect on the position chosen. The following examples relate primarily for seating arrangements in an office environment with a standard rectangular desk.

Person B can take four basic seating positions in relation to person A.

B1: The corner position.
B2: The cooperative position.
B3: The competitive/defensive position.
B4: The independent position.

The Corner Position (B1)

People who are engaged in friendly, casual conversation normally use this position. The position allows for unlimited eye contact, the opportunity to use numerous gestures and to observe the gestures of the other person. Should one person begin to feel threatened, the corner of the desk can serve as a partial barrier. The corner

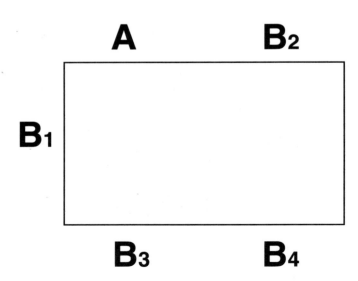

position avoids a territorial division on the top of the table and is the most successful strategic position from which a salesperson can deliver a presentation to a new customer assuming A is the buyer.

THE COOPERATIVE POSITION (B2)

This seating arrangement occurs when two people are mutually oriented, that is, they both think alike or are working on a task together. It is the most strategic position for presenting a case and having it accepted. The trick is, however, for B to be able to take this position without A feeling as though his territory has been invaded. It is also a highly successful position to take when B, the salesperson, introduces a third party into the negotiation. If a salesperson needs to have a second interview with a prospective client and has to introduce a technical expert to the client, the following strategy would be the most suitable.

The technical expert should sit at position B3 opposite customer A. The salesperson can sit either at position B2 (cooperative) or B1 (corner). This seating arrangement allows the salesperson to be 'on the client's side' and to question the technician on behalf of the client. It is known in business as 'siding with the opposition.'

THE COMPETITIVE/DEFENSIVE POSITION (B3)

Sitting across the table from a person during a negotiation creates a defensive, competitive atmosphere and can lead to each party taking a firm stand on his own point of view. The table becomes a solid barrier between both parties and allows for a distinct division of ideas. This seating arrangement is taken by people who are either competing with each other or one is reprimanding the other. It can also establish that a superior/subordinate role exists when it is used in A's office.

Research conducted in a doctor's office showed that the presence or absence of a desk had a significant effect on whether a patient was at ease or not. Only 10 percent of the patients were perceived to be at ease when the doctor's desk was present and the doctor sat behind it. This figure increased to 55 percent when the desk was absent and the doctor and patient sat side by side.

If B is seeking to persuade A, the competitive/defensive position reduces the chance of a successful negotiation unless B is deliberately sitting opposite as part of a pre-planned strategy. For example, if A is a manager who must severely reprimand employee

B, the competitive position can strengthen the reprimand. On the other hand, if B needs to make A feel superior, B can deliberately sit directly opposite A.

If your business involves dealing with people, you are in the influencing business and your objective should always be to see the other person's point of view, to put him at ease and make him feel right about dealing with you. The competitive position does not lead towards this end. More cooperation will be gained from the corner and cooperative position than will ever be achieved from the competitive position. Conversations are shorter and more specific in this position than from any other.

Two people sitting directly opposite each other across a table unconsciously divide it into two equal territories. Each claims half as his own territory and will reject the other's encroaching upon it. Similarly, two people seated competitively at a restaurant table will mark their territorial boundaries with the salt, pepper, sugar bowl and napkins.

There will be occasions on which it may be difficult or inappropriate to take the corner position to present your case. Suppose you have a visual presentation; a book or sample to present to another person who is sitting behind a rectangular desk. First, place the article on the table. The other person will either lean forward and look at it, take it into his territory or push it back into your territory.

If he leans forward to look at it, you must deliver your presentation from where you sit as his action nonverbally tells you that he does not want you on his side of the desk. If he takes it into his territory, this gives you the opportunity to ask permission to enter his territory and take either the corner or cooperative position. If, however, he pushes it back, you're in trouble! The golden rule is never to encroach on the other person's territory unless you have been given verbal or nonverbal permission to do so.

The Independent Position (B4)

This is the position taken by people when they do not wish to interact with each other; it occurs in such places as a library, cafeteria or restaurant. It signifies a lack of interest and can even be interpreted as hostile by the other person if the territorial boundaries are invaded. This position should be avoided where open discussion between A and B is required.

Square Table (Formal)

Square tables create a competitive or defensive relationship between people of equal status. Square tables are ideal for having short, to-the-point conversations or to create a superior/subordinate relationship. The most cooperation usually comes from the person seated beside you and the one on the right tends to be more cooperative than the one on the left. The most resistance, though, usually comes from the person seated directly opposite you.

Round Table (Informal)

King Arthur used the Round Table as an attempt to give each of his knights an equal amount of authority and status. A round table creates an atmosphere of relaxed informality and is ideal for promoting discussion among people who are of equal rank as each person can claim the same amount of table territory. Removing the table and sitting in a circle also promotes the same result. Unfortunately, King Arthur was unaware that if the status of one person is higher than the others in the group the round table alters the power and authority of each other individual. The king, though, held the most power at the Round Table and this meant that the knights seated on either side of him were nonverbally granted the next highest amount of power, the one on his right having a little more power than the one on the left. The amount of power diminished relative to the distance that each knight was seated away from the king.

Consequently, the knight seated directly across the table from King Arthur was, in effect, in the competitive/defensive position and was likely to be the one who gave the most trouble. Many of today's business executives use both square and round tables. The square desk, which is usually the work desk, is used for business activity, brief conversations, reprimands and the like. The round table, sometimes a coffee table with wrap-around seating, is used to create an informal relaxed atmosphere or to persuade.

Rectangular Tables

In a meeting of people of equal status the person sitting at position A at a rectangular table has the most influence, assuming that he does not have his back to the door. If A's back is facing the door, the person seated at B would be the most influential and would be

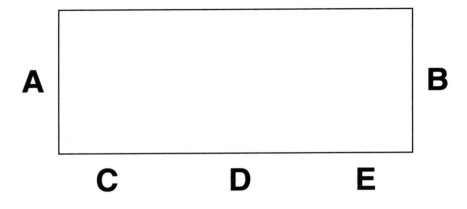

strong competition for A. Assuming that A is in the best power position, person B has the next most authority, then C, then D. This information makes it possible to structure power plays at meetings by placing name badges at the seats where you want each person to sit so that you may have the maximum influence over them.

Getting a Decision over Dinner

Bearing in mind what has already been said about human territories and the use of square, rectangular and round tables, let us now look at the dynamics of taking a person to dinner where the objective is to obtain a favorable response to a proposition. To do this we must examine the factors that can build a positive atmosphere, discuss their potential and investigate the background of man's feeding behavior.

Anthropologists tell us that man's origin was that of a tree-dweller who was strictly vegetarian, his diet consisting of roots, leaves, berries, fruit and the like. About a million years ago, he came out of the trees onto the plains to become a hunter of prey. Prior to his becoming a land dweller, man's eating habits involved continual nibbling throughout the day. Each individual was entirely responsible for his own survival and for obtaining his own food. As a hunter, however, he needed the cooperation of other individuals to capture sizeable prey, so large cooperative hunting groups were formed. Each group would leave at sunrise to hunt throughout the day and return at dusk with the day's spoils. The food was then divided equally among the hunters, who would eat inside a communal cave.

At the entrance of the cave a fire was lit to ward off dangerous animals and to provide warmth. Each caveman sat with his back against the wall of the cave to avoid the possibility of being attacked from behind while he was engrossed in eating his meal. The only sounds that were heard were the gnashing and gnawing of teeth and the crackle of the fire. This ancient process of food sharing at dusk around an open fire was the beginning of a social event that modern man reenacts in the form of barbecues, cookouts and dinner parties. He also tends to react and behave in a similar fashion at these events the same way he did over a million years ago.

At a restaurant or dinner party, a positive decision in your favor is easier to obtain when your prospect is relaxed, free of tension and his defensive barriers have been lowered. To achieve this end, and keeping in mind what has already been said about our ancestors, a few simple rules need to be followed.

First, whether you are dining at your home or at a restaurant, have your prospect seated with his back to a solid wall or screen. Research shows that respiration, heart rate, brain wave frequencies and blood pressure rapidly increase when a person sits with his back to an open space, particularly where others are moving about. Tension is further increased if the person's back is towards an open door or a window at ground level. Many top restaurants have an open fireplace or facsimile near the entrance of the restaurant to recreate the fire that burned at the ancient cave feasts. It is best to use a round table and have your prospect's view of other people obscured by a screen or large green plant if you are to have a captive audience.

It is far easier to obtain a favorable decision under these circumstances than it will ever be in restaurants that have bright lighting, tables and chairs placed in open areas, where there is banging of plates, knives and forks. Fancy restaurants use these types of relaxation techniques to extract large amounts of money from their customers' wallets for ordinary food.

Power Plays with Chairs

The height of the back of a chair raises or lowers a person's status. The higher the back of the chair, the greater the power and status of the person sitting in it. Some kings, queens and popes have the back of their throne or official chair as high as 8 feet to show their status relative to their subjects. The senior executive usually sits in a high-backed leather chair while his visitor's chair has a low back.

Swivel chairs have more power and status than fixed chairs. They also allow the user freedom of movement when he is placed under pressure and can help hide some of his nervous gestures. Chairs with arm rests, chairs that lean back and chairs that have wheels are better for negotiating power.

Chair Height

Status is gained if your chair is adjusted higher off the floor than that of your competitor. Some executives sit on high-backed chairs that are adjusted for maximum height while their visitors sit opposite, in the competitive position, on a sofa or chair that is so low that their eyes are level with the executive's desk. Another common power play is to place the visitor's low chair as far away as possible from the executive's desk into the social or public territory zone, to even further reduce his status.

Territorial and Ownership Gestures

People lean against other people or objects to show a territorial claim to that object or person. Leaning can also be used as a method of dominance or intimidation when the object that is being leaned on belongs to someone else. For example, if you are going to take a photograph of a friend and his new car or boat, you will inevitably find that he leans against his newly acquired property, putting his foot or hand on it. When he touches the property, it becomes an extension of his body and in this way he shows others that it belongs to him. Similarly, the business executive puts his feet up on his desk or desk drawers or leans against his office doorway to show his claim to his office and its furnishings.

An easy way to intimidate someone else is to lean against, sit upon or use his possessions without his permission. Leaning against the doorway of another person's office or inadvertently sitting in his chair are subtle pressure techniques.

A salesperson calling on a customer at his home is well advised to ask him, "Which seat is yours?" before he sits down, as sitting in the wrong chair intimidates the customer and puts him off. Pressure techniques have a detrimental effect on the chance of a successful sale.

Some people are habitual doorway leaners and go through life intimidating most people from the first introduction. They are well advised to practice an erect stance with palms visible to make a favorable impression on others. People form 90 percent of their opinion about you in the first ninety seconds of meeting you, and remember, you never get a second chance to make a good first impression!

Ownership Gestures

A leg-over-chair gesture reflects an easy-going, relaxed and care-free attitude, but also signifies the man's ownership of that particular chair or space. It is common to see two close friends seated this way, laughing and joking with each other, but consider the impact and meaning of this gesture in different circumstances. Suppose an employee has a personal problem and goes into the boss's office to ask his advice on a possible solution. As the employee explains his problem, he leans forward in his chair, places his hands on his knees, puts his face down and looks dejected. The boss listens intently, sitting motionless, then suddenly leans back in his chair and puts one leg over the arm of his chair. In this circumstance the boss's attitude seems to immediately change to a lack of concern or indifference. In other words, he is showing little empathy for the employee or his problem and may even feel that his time is being wasted with the 'same old story.'

If the boss's chair has no arms (which is unlikely; this is usually the visitor's chair), his ownership gesture may be to put one or both of his feet on his desk. If his superior enters his office, it is unlikely that the boss would use such an obvious territorial/ownership gesture, but would resort to more subtle versions, perhaps putting his foot on the bottom drawer of his desk, or placing his foot hard against the leg of the desk to stake his claim to it.

These gestures can be quite annoying if they occur during negotiation. It is vital that the person change to a different position. The longer a person stays in the leg-over-chair or feet-on-desk position, the longer he will have an indifferent or hostile attitude. An easy way to break someone from this gesture is to hand him something that he cannot reach and ask him to lean across and look at it. Or, if you and he have a similar sense of humor, tell him he has a split in his trousers.

Strategic Office Layout

Your office furniture should be arranged in such a way that you can have as much power, status or control over others as you wish. Just sitting behind a desk conveys a sense of power and positioning it so that all who enter must look across it to you suggests control. On the other hand, to create an accessible, open door image, situate your desk so that your back is to the door and that you must turn around to greet your visitors. This way there is nothing standing between the two of you. The texture of furniture can also set up status; a wooden desk gives off an entirely different impression than a metal desk does.

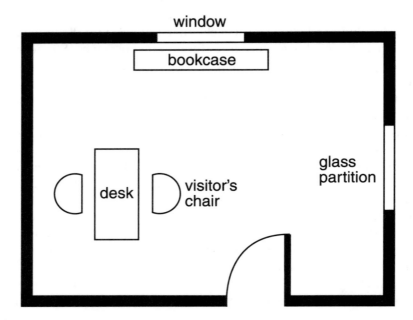

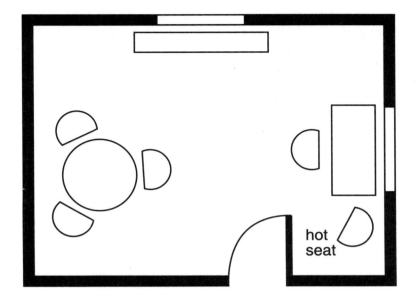

Certain objects strategically placed around the office can be used to increase the status and power of the occupant. Some examples include:

1. Low sofas for visitors to sit on.
2. A wall covered with photos, awards or qualifications that the occupant has received.
3. A slim briefcase. Those who do all the work carry large, bulky briefcases.
4. An expensive ashtray placed out of the reach of the visitor causing him inconvenience when ashing his cigarette.
5. Some red folders placed on the desk marked 'Strictly Confidential.'

If a supervisor keeps an employee waiting a long time (more than 15 minutes), devotes only a short time to the meeting when a longer conference is appropriate and meets only occasionally with the employee, then the supervisor is communicating a negative, disrespectful attitude toward that employee.

During a sales call, massive desks not only provide the client with a physical barrier, they serve as a visual barrier as well. If you can't see him from the chest down, how do you know if the buyer's legs are crossed, if he's tapping his foot or cleaning his nails.

It is best, therefore, to choose a chair that is beside the buyer's desk rather than one across from it. In order to see you better, the buyer will turn towards you forcing him to move away from his desk and thus expose all of his nonverbal communication channels to you.

Personal Selling Power: Basis for a Successful Close

Preparing for a sales call is not limited to thinking about the coming meeting while you're waiting in the client's office. Just as you can practice your presentation well before the call, you need to consider the type of visual impression you will make on your client as well.

A client needs to decide, in a short amount of time, whether you are reliable, truthful and professional. Even before you verbally greet the client, you should analyze your clothing, your posture and your neatness, because they all indicate to others how you feel about your job. Here are a few tips for creating a positive first impression that can make what you say—with your words, your tone of voice and your body language—much more effective.

1. Dress conservatively: Each area of sales has a uniform, from Wall Street pin stripe to Record Store Khakis and sports coat. Outlandish fashions may catch the client's attention, but they'll leave a *negative* impression.
2. Colors create an image: Solid suits of gray, beige and navy blue for men, and two-piece dresses with jackets or a suit in similar colors for women are basics. Avoid aggressive colors like orange or turquoise, and any color that doesn't suit your hair, eye and skin color.
3. Neatness counts: Attention to the details of your clothing, such as a well-pressed shirt and polished shoes, tell the customer that you're conscientious. A disheveled appearance gives the impression of disorganization and carelessness.
4. Quality is the key: No matter what the price of your suit or dress, get a good tailoring job. Watch accessories; ties, jewelry and attaché cases that are tacky can ruin your overall image.
5. Stand tall: Good posture and a confident stride indicate that you are happy and capable. Slouching or a shuffling gait can convey an 'I don't care about what I'm doing' attitude, and will make a well-tailored outfit hang poorly.

When you realize that the deciding factor for a sale could rest on your client's visual impression of you, doesn't it make sense to project the very best image possible?

Use an Effective Waiting Posture

Before you see your client, you will probably have to wait in a lobby, a reception room or an assistant's office. Take care to monitor your nonverbal behavior while you're deep in thought because office insiders are sure to notice you while you're in their territory. An efficient, observant secretary will be aware of your waiting posture and make a mental note of it—either positive or negative.

Sit in a comfortable, encouraging and composed posture. Then take a quick five-channel scan of yourself. Make sure that you aren't reinforcing your feelings of tension by using negative body language. Then:

1. Relax.
2. Use creative imagery, think positive thoughts.
3. Check over your appearance.
4. Resist visualizing your client as 'just like you.' Be prepared to bridge the differences between you and your potential customer.
5. Remind yourself that maximum flexibility will translate into maximum potential.
6. SMILE!

Your Basic Listening Posture

You are more likely to use a good listening posture if you have one ready to put into action. Showing your client that you are paying attention while he is answering your questions is very important. It encourages him to continue talking, thus giving you additional information. Keep in mind the following gestures that help to convey your interest and use the ones that you feel most comfortable with.

1. Tilt your head slightly.
2. Nod as major points are mentioned or in rhythm with the client's speech pattern.
3. Lean a bit back in your chair with your head raised slightly—make sure to keep your arms and hands open and move them in a positive manner as you stress your points.
4. Maintain good eye contact; a slight squint shows that you are considering what is being said.
5. Avoid self-touching gestures—although clients may use chin rubbing, lip pulling and cheek tapping when they are evaluating your statements, these gestures can also express uncertainty.
6. Prevent yourself from frowning.
7. Take notes—unless you have an excellent memory for details, you should jot down the client's needs, motivations and concerns.

Closing

Closing requires confidence and the conviction that your product or service is worth more than the price you're asking the prospect to pay. Top salespeople consistently show two behavior characteristics that get them the sale: the capacity to be friendly (empathy opens the sale) and the ability to be firm (ego drive closes the sale).

Although these attitudes may be present in every salesperson, they need to be applied in equal measure. Salespeople who are too friendly will get along fine with the customer, and will easily get a whole series of positive signals, but may lack the inner strength to ask for the order. Salespeople who are too firm, on the other hand, may bulldoze through a sale, annoy the prospect and cause unnecessary changes from positive to negative signals.

The ability to be friendly and to create positive signals is only a means to an end—the sale, the satisfied need, the happy customer and your satisfied ego. To turn positive signals into dollars, you need to balance this friendliness with firmness to close the sale.

1. Use a first trial close as soon as you notice several positive signals.
2. Never try to close when the customer signals uncertainty gestures.
3. Express 'buy from me' signals during the close.
4. Move closer to your customer by leaning forward, increase your eye contact with him and use head nods to seal the deal.

Visual, Auditory and Action Closes

By the time you have reached the closing phase of your sales call, you will know the type of language and information a client prefers to use and hear. If you have been matching your vocabulary to your customer's, a close stressing this preference will seem natural.

VISUAL CLOSES: These are the 'show and tell' type of closes. Using pen and paper, you demonstrate in black and white how your prospect will benefit from purchasing your product. When the customer signals that he is ready and after he has listened to several benefit statements, look at the client, pick up a pen and pad and say, "I'd like us to take a moment to review what we've discussed," then list the benefits that the new product would provide for his operation.

Another way to appeal to the visual buyer involves a written summary of the pros and cons of his buying decision. Draw a solid vertical line to divide a paper into two parts and say, "Here on the left side, we'll list the benefits that we've already discussed such as higher productivity (look at the customer, nod your head), lower downtime (look at the customer and smile), and the fact that you'll save approximately 14 percent on operating costs (make eye contact, then pause). Which one of these benefits would be the most important one for you?"

AUDITORY CLOSES: Prospects who prefer an auditory vocabulary and information are most likely to buy from you when your close involves decision-making statements or asking questions to which the only reasonable answer is 'Yes.' Examples are: "Do you like the quality of this storage building?" "Do you like the colors you selected earlier?"

This repeated 'Yes' mode has a powerful psychological impact on the auditory customer. Each additional 'Yes' increases his subconscious desire to repeat the positive internal experience of the 'Yes' sound. Top sales producers know the benefit from this phenomenon and obtain several 'Yes' responses before they ask for the order.

The extra incentive close for the auditory buyer involves you making your offer sound irresistible by verbalizing it with excitement in your voice. Saying: "We have only two units left (right hand-to-chest gesture) and we're providing a special two-hour training course for your personnel with the purchase of this new system (smile)," with enthusiasm in your voice, perks his attention.

The alternate-choice close is another method of close that appeals to the auditory buyer. To lead your customer from a thinking mode to a decision mode, ask a question about the details of your proposal. Asking, "Does this lease plan sound good to you or would you like to hear about owning this equipment?" forces him to make a judgment decision.

ACTION CLOSES: Action-oriented prospects show a number of 'I am ready to buy' signals early in the sales presentation. Signals such as:

- Nodding their head up and down.
- Making physical contact with you (i.e., placing a hand on your shoulder).
- Rubbing their hands together.
- Grabbing a pen for writing.
- Walking around your product, stroking parts of it (feeling the paint, adjusting the seat, opening the trunk, etc.).

Action-oriented buyers love to give you a hand; therefore, ask them to do things to help you with the demonstration. Since they like motion, prospects who use action-oriented language respond well to your leadership. If you've made a product presentation outside and realize that the prospect is still undecided, you could say: "Mrs. Phillips, let's take a moment and walk over to the office (start moving, continue talking as you walk)." "I'd like you to take a look at two large photographs of similar designs which I think will really suit your specific needs."

Sometimes your customer may be ready for the purchase, but needs a gentle push to make the decision. You, on the other hand, know that too much assertiveness may be counterproductive.

When this happens, begin packing up your sales literature, order forms and samples, leading the customer to believe that you are on your way out the door. Soon you'll see your prospect's defenses being lowered. As you notice these signals, turn to the customer and refocus on the dominant buying motive. Save a good product feature, a special finance offer, an extra incentive or a new creative solution to the client's problem for the pack-up-and-leave close. Your moving closer to the customer's door lowers his resistance to a successful comeback and final close.

Basics for a Successful Close

When you have used 100 percent of your communication abilities during a sales call, your close should follow automatically. Getting to the close means that you have managed your own and your client's body language effectively. To conclude your meeting successfully you should:

- Avoid beginning a close unless you have positive buying signals from your client.
- Continue to use your own open, encouraging signals and maintain good eye contact.
- Select a close that suits your client based on his preference for visual, auditory or action words and information.
- Immediately redirect your approach if the client signals doubt during your close—ask open questions, restate benefits and continue to respond with positive, supportive signals.
- Smile and thank the client for the order.
- Reassure the buyer that the order is only the beginning of a long-term relationship.

- Schedule a follow-up call to check on how his purchase has improved his business operation or personal situation.

The Rules of Nonverbal Selling Power
FIRST MEETINGS

Rule 1: Manage every second of a first meeting. Do not delude yourself that a bad impression can be easily corrected. Putting things right is a lot harder than getting them right the first time.

Rule 2: Always initiate the eyebrow flash (shows friendliness, approval or agreement) whenever possible. Be certain to respond to another's eyebrow flash unless your calculated intention is to signal hostility.

Rule 3: Break eye contact downward, unless it is your deliberate intention to convey a lack of interest in the other person or to throw him temporarily off balance by a disconcerting upward eye break.

Rule 4: Never hold a gaze for more than three seconds when first meeting someone. Look, then break eye contact briefly. Even though the person receiving the message is unable to explain the reason for his feelings, any violation of this rule can generate a negative impression. The only exception to this rule is during a power play when it is your deliberate intention to distress your opponent.

Rule 5: Use the smile most suitable to the situation. Smiling inappropriately can create as negative an impression as not smiling at all.

USING SPACE—WHILE STANDING

Rule 6: Never invade another person's intimate zone unintentionally. If you do so deliberately, as a power-play strategy, be aware that you will provoke a powerful increase in negative arousal.

Rule 7: Be certain that you are working at the correct spatial distance to achieve the results you require. Take into account individual and cultural differences, as well as the nature of the relationship. Learn to work at a variety of distances without feeling alienated or uneasy. The more flexible you can be in manipulating another person's various zones, the greater control you will be able to exert over the encounter.

Rule 8: Never stand directly opposite an unknown male or adjacent to an unfamiliar female. With a man, start at a more side-on position and gradually work your way around to a more frontal one. With a woman, adopt the opposite approach by starting the encounter in a frontal position and then moving slowly to a more adjacent one.

Rule 9: Never stand when someone else is sitting, unless it is your intention to dominate or intimidate the other person. Height is a powerful authority signal.

Rule 10: Avoid, if possible, deep arm chairs that compel you to sit far back. Sitting in this type of chair limits your ability to send out a number of important posture signals.

Rule 11: When chairs can be moved, the rules for personal distance apply. You can get away with sitting closer to another person than you could if standing, because the chair increases your sense of security and its arms provide a physical barrier between you and the other person.

WHILE SHAKING HANDS

Rule 12: Keep your hands dry and apply a moderate amount of pressure when shaking hands. Limit the handshake to three pumps and hold the handshake for approximately six seconds—under most circumstances.

Rule 13: To communicate dominance, use the palm-down handshake. To convey friendship and a desire for cooperation, use the vertical handshake. To convey submission, employ the palm-up handshake.

Rule 14: To avoid looking dishonest, stay away from wearing tinted, dark or reflecting glasses.

Rule 15: To increase the warmth and impact of your presence when first meeting someone, use a head tilt, direct eye contact until you remember their eye color and a warm smile. Use the same gesture whenever you are asking for help or cooperation.

Rule 16: When speaking to a group, ensure that your gaze includes them all. Avoid reading from a script; either memorize what you wish to say or use brief notes.

POWER PLAYS

Rule 17: A successful power play depends on your ability to control the other person's time and space.

Rule 18: Walk slowly, walk deliberately and walk tall. Take the time to review your surroundings. Adopt the manner of a proprietor, not the cautious air of someone who doesn't really belong there. Imagine that you own the place and move accordingly. Never allow yourself to be hurried.

Rule 19: Whenever possible, choose where and how you sit. Select a chair that is easy to get in and out of. Avoid the trap of a deep and confining punishment chair.

Rule 20: Your ability to dominate others can be enhanced by a deliberate invasion of their personal space.

Rule 21: To dominate another person, first take control of his time. The longer you compel them to wait—up to a point—the greater the dominance you demonstrate. Use the fifteen-minute test. If he is still patiently waiting for the meeting after that time, you will have dominated him to the point where his perceived status is significantly undermined.

Rule 22: Stick to the fifteen-minute rule for being kept waiting. At the end of this period, unless there is an obviously valid and genuine reason for the delay, abort the meeting.

READING OTHERS

Rule 23: Detect anxiety in another person by looking at his feet and his hands rather than his face. Watch for his body language 'leakage' gestures, as his small subconscious, controlled movements relieve his inner tensions.

Rule 24: No matter what you are trying to sell, silent speech buying signs tell you if the other person wants to make a deal. Key signs to watch for are: a sudden release of tension (sigh), intensified eye contact, greater proximity and increased chin touching.

Rule 25: Liars betray themselves in several ways. Watch for increased self-touching that involves rubbing or stroking the ears, nose or eyes. Aggressive, forced movements of the feet, hands or mouth can detect deceptions involving hostility.

Conclusion

Sales success is a combination of three factors: knowledge, skills and motivation. To translate knowledge into action skills, you need to practice, make mistakes, learn from them and grow. New action skills will increase your confidence tremendously and boost your motivation to an all-time high.

Study each picture sequence that follows and see what body language gestures you can interpret from what you have read in this book. You will be amazed to find how much your perceptiveness has improved.

1. Can you spot the liar?
2. Which man is holding back his opinion?
3. Which of the three shows the most disapproval and disinterest?
4. Who is the most defensive of the three? What gestures show this?
5. What lack-of-concern gesture do you see in this picture?

1. What four open and honest gestures can you identify from the man on the left?
2. What two defensive gestures are being used by the woman?
3. Can you spot the confident or superior gesture in the picture?
4. Who is using the critical evaluation gesture?
5. Who is the most argumentative and why?

If you haven't started your program of nonverbal selling power yet, here are some pointers to use as a guideline for improving your sales techniques.

- Watch what people do with their bodies every day for a week. You may want to use the five nonverbal communication channels as a starter—concentrate on Body Angle on Monday, Faces on Tuesday, Arms on Wednesday, Hands on Thursday and Leg Postures on Friday.
- Improve your nonverbal observation skills by watching TV interviews with the sound off. Note the guest's initial seating position (usually legs crossed away from the host), and the

hand gestures (the confident guest uses frequent, open gestures). Also note the 'mirroring' effect when both people are on the same wavelength (positive or negative).

- Imitate gestures you've seen in a client's office, after the call, in order to 'feel and understand' what your customer has expressed nonverbally.
- Work on your listening posture, your opening seating position and your ability to express positive signals no matter what objections you hear.
- Ask your colleagues to role-play in small groups with you. Form triads (3 people per group), one plays the role of the buyer, one plays the seller and the third acts as observer. Learn to apply new techniques in a safe, controlled situation before you use them on a real customer.
- Develop a 'nonverbal call report' diary to use after your sales call. Write down what type of nonverbal signals you used on calls where you got the order and what signals you used when you lost a sale. Your own observations may be a bit too self-critical, but soon you'll see a pattern of success in your approach. Follow it. Your goal is to identify the characteristics of your own best performance and repeat them often.
- Finally, learn how to use verbal and nonverbal selling power simultaneously. Start by persuasive eye contact as you translate product features into customer benefits. Apply one new skill each day. Practice, practice, practice.

You have been reacting to nonverbal communication signals and sending out your body language messages all your life. Responding to these signals in a positive manner, instead of reacting to them in a negative way, will provide you with an enormous competitive edge. You've just added 93 percent to your communication potential. Putting *Strictly Business Body Language* to work will turn that potential into profit.

Bibliography

Axtell, Roger E., *Gestures*, John Wiley & Sons, Inc., New York, 1998.

Beier, Ernest G. and Valens, Evans G., *People Reading*, Scarborough House, Maryland, 1992.

Birdwhistell, Ray, *Introduction to Kinesics*, University of Louisville Press, Kentucky, 1952.

Birdwhistell, Ray, *Kinesics and Context*, University of Pennsylvania Press, Pennsylvania, 1970.

Carnegie, Dale, *How to Win Friends and Influence People*, Simon and Schuster, New York, 1937.

Darwin, Charles, *The Expression of Emotion in Man and Animals*, Appleton-Century-Crofis, New York, 1872.

Dimitrius, Jo-Ellan, *Reading People*, Random House, Inc., New York, 1998.

Dimitrius, Jo-Ellan and Mazzarella, Mark, *Put Your Best Foot Forward*, Simon and Schuster, New York, 2000.

Dunkell, Samuel, *Sleep Positions*, New American Library, New York, 1978.

Ekman, Paul, *Darwin and Facial Expressions*, Academic Press, New York, 1973.

Ekman, Paul, Friesen, W. and Ellsworth, P., *Emotion of the Human Face*, Pergamon Press, New York, 1972.

Ekman, Paul, *Telling Lies*, W. W. Norton & Company, New York, 1992.

Ekman, Paul, and Friesen, W., *Unmasking the Face*, Prentice-Hall, New Jersey, 1975.

Fast, Julius, *Body Language*, Simon and Schuster, New York, 1970.

Fast, Julius, *Subtext*, Viking Publishers, New York, 1991.

Goldman, Daniel, *Vital Lies, Simple Truths*, Simon and Schuster, New York, 1985.

Gschwandtner, Gerhad, *Nonverbal Selling Power*, Prentice Hall, Inc., New Jersey, 1985.

Hargrave, Jan, *Let Me See Your Body Talk*, Kendall/Hunt Publishing Company, Iowa, 1995.

Hargrave, Jan and Weiser, Alice, *Judge The Jury*, Kendall/Hunt Publishing Company, 2000.

Kuei, Chi An, *Face Reading*, Souvenir Press Ltd., London, 1998.

Lewis, David, *The Secret Language of Success*, Carroll & Graff Publishers, Inc., New York, 1989.

McKay, Matther, Davis, Martha and Fanning, Patrick, *Messages*, New Harbor Publications, California, 1995.

Mehrabian, Albert, *Silent Messages*, Wadsworth, Belmont, California, 1971.

Mehrabian, Albert, *Tactics of Social Influence*, Prentice-Hall, New Jersey, 1969.

Morris, Desmond, *Body Talk*, Crown Publishers, Inc., New York, 1994.

Morris, Desmond, *The Naked Ape*, McGraw-Hill, New York, 1968.

Morris, Desmond, *Intimate Behavior*, Cape, London, 1971.

Morris, Desmond, *Manwatching*, Abrams, New York, 1977.

Morrison, Tern, Conaway, Wayne A. and Borden, George A., *Kiss, Bow, or Shake Hands*, Adams Media Corporation, Massachusetts, 1994.

Nierrenberg, Gerald and Calero, H., *How to Read a Person Like a Book*, Hawthorn Books, New York, 1971

Pease, Allan, *Signals*, Bantam Books, Inc., Canada, 1984.

Tannen, Deborah, *Talking from 9 to 5*, William Morrow and Company, New York, 1994.

Wainwright, Gordon R., *Body Language*, NTC Publishing Group, Chicago, 1993.